iii

Contents

Contents

Contents

Contents

Contents

Contents

Preface

This book grew out partly of lectures to undergraduate students of information technology and other related topics within the curriculum of the undergraduates of the mathematical sciences. Due to lack of simple text book dealing solely with mathematics for computing, the author tried to work out a text book to serve as a simple and good reference for the students, to master the topic and develop a good basis for further reading. Very often the students complain from the complexity and diversity of text books they need to go through. The book is intended to develop knowledge of the Mathematics upon which computer science and information technology are based. The book stresses, basic principals, avoid using intensive math where possible, and maintain simplicity for students to understand. Large collection of exercises and solutions are included to help students to develop skills for problem solving and grasp the subject.

Topics covered include number systems, computer arithmetic, logic, Boolean algebra, matrix algebra and basic topics in numerical analysis.

M. M. Yousif

1 Number, Arithmetic and Number systems.

1.1 Prime numbers

Integer p is called prime number [1] if p is > 1 and has no +ve divisors other than 1 and itself. If we have the sequence 2,3,4,5,.... and would like to select the prime numbers from the sequence, we first discard multiple of two, then we discard multiples of three and continuing this process, we find the sequence of primes 2,3,5,7,11,.... by eliminating all multiples.

1.2 Integers

Integers[2] are whole numbers, including zero and negative values, e.g. ..., -2, -1, 0, 1, 2, ... (integers)   1, 2, 3, 4, ... (positive integers)
 0, 1, 2, 3, 4, ... (nonnegative integers)
 0, -1, -2, -3, -4, ... (nonpositive integers)
-1, -2, -3, -4, ... (negative integers)

1.3 Rational numbers

Rational numbers include integers and all other numbers that can be expressed as the quotient of two integers, e.g. ½, -3/5, 55/21, 5.

1.4 Irrational numbers

Numbers that cannot be expressed as the quotient of two integers are called irrational numbers, e.g. $\sqrt{2}$, $\sqrt{5}$, π, e.

1.5   Real numbers

The field (any set of elements that satisfies the field axioms [3] for both addition and multiplication) of all rational and irrational numbers is called the real numbers, and denoted by $\Re$. The real numbers can be extended with the addition of the imaginary number i, equal to $\sqrt{-1}$. Numbers of the form x +iy, where x and y are both real, are called complex numbers, which also form a field.

1.6   Complex numbers

The complex numbers are numbers of the form x + iy, where x and y are real numbers and i is the imaginary unit equal to the square root of -1, e.g. 2-i$\sqrt{2}$,

1.7   Imaginary numbers

Imaginary numbers do not belong to real numbers such as $\sqrt{-2}$.

1.8   Ordinal Number

In common usage, an ordinal number is an adjective which describes the numerical position of an object, e.g., first, second, third, etc.

1.9   Cardinal Number

In common usage, a cardinal number is a number used in counting (a counting number), such as 1, 2, 3, ...
A cardinal number is a type of number defined in such a way that any method of counting sets using it gives the same result. (This is

not true for the ordinal numbers.) In fact, the cardinal numbers are obtained by collecting all ordinal numbers which are obtainable by counting a given set. The cardinality of a set A is denoted by |A| and is the total number of elements in the set.

1.10 Decimal

Decimal is the base-10 notational system for representing real numbers. The expression of a number using the decimal system is called its decimal expansion, examples of which include 1, 13, 2028, 12.1, and 3.14159. Each of the Arabic numerals 0 to 9 is called a decimal digit, and the period placed to the right of the units place in a decimal number is called the decimal point (or, in the case that a comma is instead used for this purpose as is the case in continental Europe, the decimal comma).

1.11 Arithmetic

Arithmetic is the branch of mathematics dealing with integers or, more generally, numerical computation. Arithmetical operations include addition, congruence calculation (Modular arithmetic), division, factorization, multiplication, power computation, root extraction, and subtraction. If two numbers b and c have the property that their difference b-c is integrally divisible by a number m, then b and c are said to be "congruent modulo m." The number m is called the modulus, and the statement "b is congruent to c (modulo m)" is written mathematically as $b \equiv c \pmod{m}$

1.12 Relative and absolute errors

If y approximates x, then |y-x| is the absolute error. The relative error is given by |y-x|/|x| where x is not equal to zero. The relative error is expressed in % by multiplying by 100. The relative error is more meaningful than the absolute error as we can see from the following examples.

Examples:

a.   x = 3.0 ,y = 3.1
        Absolute error = 0.1 and relative error = 0.03333
b.   x = 0.0003 , y = 0.00031
        Absolute error = 0.00001 and relative error = 0.03333
c.   x = 3000 ,y = 3100
        Absolute error = 100 and relative error = 0.03333

Note: In the above examples while we get the same relative errors, the absolute errors are varying, which may be misleading.

1.13 Precision and accuracy

The precision of a decimal number is given by the position of the right most significant digit and the accuracy is given by the number of significant digits in the number. As an example the number 1.345 is accurate to four significant digits and is set with a precision to the nearest thousandth.

1.14 Fundamental Theorem of Arithmetic.

The fundamental theorem of arithmetic states that every positive integer (except the number 1) can be represented in exactly one way (one and only) apart from rearrangement as a product of one or more primes. This theorem is also called the unique factorization theorem. The fundamental theorem of arithmetic is a corollary of the first of Euclid's theorems[4]

1.15 Computer Arithmetic.

Floating-point arithmetic is the arithmetic performed on real numbers by computers or other automated devices using a fixed number of bits.

1.15.1 Machine numbers

Machine numbers are of two kinds. These are floating-point and fixed-point. The floating-point is equivalent the notation in the decimal system, where a number is written as a decimal fraction times an integral power of 10. For example 133.456 could be represented as 1.33456 x 10^2. All computer instructions and data are represented and stored in binary (base 2) form. In the representation of fixed-point numbers, the value of each digit in the number depends on its position relative to the fixed decimal point. For example the integer value 53 in base 10 is represented by the binary or base 2 value 00110101, denoted by

$53_{10} = 00110101_2$

in base 10, this means

$53_{10} = 5 \times 10^1 + 3 \times 10^0$

Similarly,

$00110101_2 = 0 \times 2^7 + 0 \times 2^6 + 1 \times 2^5 + 1 \times 2^4 + 0 \times 2^3 + 1 \times 2^2 + 0 \times 2^1 + 1 \times 2^0$

$= 32_{10} + 16_{10} + 4_{10} + 1_{10}$

Thus, each bit position represents an increasing power of 2, beginning with 2^0 on the right. The fixed point allows for fraction. In general the floating point is written as

$\pm F \times B^E$,

Where F (fraction) is the mantissa, B is the base of the number and E (an integer) is the exponent. The floating number is normalised when the leading digit is non-zero. For example

35.72×10^2 is not normalised and,

0.3572×10^2 is normalised.

The real number, say y, is approximated by a machine as $fl(y)$ by chopping (remove digits d_{k+1} , d_{k+1} ...) or rounding (if d_{k+1} <5 chopping and if d_{k+1} >5 , round d_k by adding 1)

Example: if y= 3.14159265... = $.314159265...\times 10^1$

6-digit chopping would give: $fl(y) = .314159\times 10^1$

6-digit rounding would give: $fl(y) = .314159\times 10^1$

4-digit chopping would give: $fl(y) = .3141\times 10^1$

4-digit rounding would give: $fl(y) = .3142\times 10^1$

Let x, y be real numbers and $fl(x)$, $fl(y)$ (floating numbers) are machine numbers representing x and y. The basic operations of computer addition, subtraction, multiplication and division are carried out as follows:

a. $x + y = fl\ (fl(x) + fl(y))$

b. $x - y = fl\ (fl(x) - fl(y))$

c. $x \times y = fl\ (fl(x) \times fl(y))$

d. $x \div y = fl\ (fl(x) \div fl(y))$.

Example:

For x= 2/3 and y=5/7, perform the above operations.

a. $x = .666666....\times 10^0$

$y = .7142857...\times 10^0$ normalised

$fl(x) = .66666\times 10^0$

$fl(y) = .71428\times 10^0$ 5 digit chopping

$x + y = fl\ (.66666\times 10^0 + .71428\times 10^0)$

$= fl\ (1.38094\times 10^0)$

$= fl\ (.138094\times 10^1) = .138094\times 10^1$

The exact value = 2/3 + 5/7 = 29/21 = 1.38952

The relative error = .896552E-05

b. $x - y = fl\ (.66666\times 10^0 - .71428\times 10^0)$

$= fl\ (-.04762\times 10^0)$

$= -.04762\times 10^0$

The exact value = 2/3 - 5/7 = -1/21 = -0.04762

The relative error = -.2E-04

c. $x \times y = fl\,(.66666 \times 10^0 \times .71428 \times 10^0)$
$= fl\,(0.476182 \times 10^0)$
$= 0.476182 \times 10^0$
The exact value $= 2/3 \times 5/7 = 10/21 = 0.47169$
The relative error $= 0.178E\text{-}04$

d. $x \div y = fl\,(.66666 \times 10^0 \div .71428 \times 10^0)$
$= fl\,(0.933331 \times 10^0)$
$= 0.933331 \times 10^0$
The exact value $= 2/3 \div 5/7 = 14/15 = 0.933333$
The relative error $= 0.200002E\text{-}05$

Several of the usual laws of arithmetic do not hold in computer arithmetic. As the following example shows, the associate law of addition does hold for computer addition.

Example: let x=0.355, y=7.59 and z = 42.4 using 3-digit chopping. The exact value of summing x,y and z is 50.345.

The associative law is: $x + (y+z) = (x+y)+z$

Now we have $x + (y+z) = 0.355 + (7.59 + 42.4) = 0.355 + 49.9$
$fl(50.255) = fl(.50255 \times 10^2)$
$= .502 \times 10^2 = 50.2$ (1)

The absolute error$= 50.345 - 50.2 = 0.145$
and $(x+y)+z = 7.945 + 42.4 = fl(50.34) = fl(.5034 \times 10^2)$
$= .503 \times 10^2 = 50.3$ (2)

The absolute error$= 50.345 - 50.3 = 0.045$

(1) and (2) are unequal, and therefore the addition is not associative. (1) has the largest error.

Calculation involving subtraction of nearly equal numbers, in general, leads to a build up of round off errors. To avoid such cancellation of errors let us look at the following example.

Find the roots of $ax^2 + bx + c = 0$, given that a $\neq 0$ and $b^2 > 4ac$.

The real roots are: $x_1 = (-b + \sqrt{b^2 - 4ac}\,)/2a$

$x_2 = (-b - \sqrt{b^2 - 4ac}\,)/2a$

For $b = 62.10$, $a = 1$ and $c = 1$, the exact roots are:

$$x_1 = -0.01610723$$
$$x_2 = -62.08390$$
$$\text{fl}(a) = .1000 \times 10^1$$
$$\text{fl}(b) = .6210 \times 10^2$$
$$\text{fl}(c) = .1000 \times 10^1$$

Machine value of $\sqrt{b^2 - 4ac} = .6206 \times 10^2$

$\text{fl}(x_1) = \text{fl}(-0.04/2) = -.2 \times 10^{-1}$, with relative error of $0.24167842..$ or approximately 24%.

Similarly $\text{fl}(x_2) = \text{fl}(-62.1) = .621 \times 10^2$, with relative error of 0.00032 or approximately .032%.

Calculation of x_1 leads cancellation of errors, since $-b + \sqrt{b^2 - 4ac} \approx -b + b$ (subtraction of approximately equal numbers).

This is valid when $\sqrt{b^2 - 4ac} \approx b$. On the other hand, x_2 involves $-b - \sqrt{b^2 - 4ac} \approx -(b + b)$, i.e. addition and therefore no cancellation problems. To avoid error cancellation, we adjust the formula for x_1 as follows:

$$x_1 = (-b + \sqrt{b^2 - 4ac})/2a =$$

$$(-b + \sqrt{b^2 - 4ac})(-b - \sqrt{b^2 - 4ac})/2a \,(-b - \sqrt{b^2 - 4ac}) =$$

$$(b^2 - \sqrt{b^2 - 4ac})/2a \,(-b - \sqrt{b^2 - 4ac}) = -2c/(b + \sqrt{b^2 - 4ac}).$$

Then $x_1 = c/a\, x_2$.

In calculating the roots of the quadratic, x_2 should be calculated first from $x_2 = (-b - \sqrt{b^2 - 4ac})/2a$ and then, $x_1 = c/a\, x_2$.

The base 2 method of counting in which only the digits 0 and 1 (binary digits) are used, in this base, the number 1011 equals $1.2^0+1.2^1+0.2^2+1.2^3=11$. This base is used in computers, since all numbers can be simply represented as a string of electrically pulsed ons and offs. One binary digit is called a bit, and eight digits are called a byte.

1.15.2 Binary numbers

Computers use binary representation of numbers instead of decimal system. In the decimal system we use 10 (referred to as radix of the decimal system) as a base and there are 10 different digits, 0,1,2,3,4,5,6,7,8,9. Numbers are represented as a sequence of these digits. A number written in radix 2 (binary system) contains two digits, 0 and 1 and each digit is called a bit. Such number can be represented by a sequence of switches or other devices with two states corresponding to 0 and 1.Fractions may also be introduced in the binary system, by considering negative powers of 2. For example $^3/4$ in decimal system is written as 0.75 and in binary system is written as 0.11, meaning $1(2^{-1}) + 1(2^{-2})$.

-        Decimal system: $635 = 6* 10^2+3 * 10^1+5 * 10^0$
-        Binary system: $1101, = 1*2^4+1 *2^3+0*2^3+1*2^1+1*2^0$

1.15.2.1 Converting a number from a decimal system to the system of radix R

In general $N=a_kR^k+...+a_2R^2+a_1R+a_o$

Method 1:

To convert any number N from the decimal system to the system with radix R, the following steps are followed:

1- Determine the highest power, k, of R which does not exceed N. Divide N by R^k. The quotient, a_k, is the first digit of N and the remainder, r_1, is used in the following step.

2- Divide N by R^k. The quotient, a_k, is the first digit of N and the remainder, r_1, is used in the following step.

3- If r_1 is larger than R^{k-1}, divide r_1, by R^{k-1} to obtain a quotient a_{k-1}, the second digit of N, and the remainder r_2 to be used in the following step. If r_1 is smaller than R^{k-1}, the second digit of N is 0, and r_1, is used in the following step.

4- Repeat step 3 with the result of 3 and continue until all powers of R less than k have been used.

Example 1:

Covert N = 97 with R = 3

$R^4 = 3^4 = 81$

$97/81 = 1$ (a_4), and $r_1 = 16$ .... 1st digit = **1**

$R^{k-1} = 3^3 = 27 > 16$ .... 2nd digit = **0**

$16/9 = 1$ (a_3), and $r_3 = 7 < 9$ 3rd digit = **1**

$R^{k-3} = 3^1 = 3$

$7/3 = 2$ (a_2), and $r_2 = 1 < 7$ 4th digit = **2**

$R^{k-4} = 3^0 = 1$

$1/1 = 1$ (a^0) ...   . 5th digit = **1**

Thus, **10121** is the number system with radix 3.

Example 2:

Convert the number 14 to binary number (R = 2)

- $R^3 = 2^3 = 8$
- $14/8 = 1$ (a_3), and $r_1 = 6$ ...... 1st digit = **1**
- $R^{k-1} = 2^2 = 4 < 6$ ....
- $6/4 = 1$ (a_3), and $r_2 = 2$ 2nd digit = **1**
- $R^{k-2} = 2^1 = 2$
- $2/2 = 1$ (a_2), and $r_2 = 0$ 3rd digit = **1**
- $R^{k-3} = 2^0 = 1 > 0$ 4th digit = **0**

Thus, the binary number for 14 is **1110**.

Method 2:

Divide the number by 2, then divide what's left by 2, and so on until there is nothing left (0). Write down the remainder (which is either 0 or 1) at each division stage. Once there are no more divisions, list the remainder values in reverse order. This is the binary equivalent.

Examples:

Using method 2, convert the numbers 14 and 97 to   binary number

    14/2=7   with a remainder of 0
    7/2=3   with a remainder of 1
    3/2=1   with a remainder of 1
    ½=0   with a remainder of 1

Thus, the binary number for 14 is **1110**.

    97/2=48   with a remainder of 1
    48/2=24   with a remainder of 0
    24/2=12   with a remainder of 0
    12/2=6   with a remainder of 0
    6/2=3   with a remainder of 0
    3/2=1   with a remainder of 1
    1/2=0   with a remainder of 1

Thus, the binary number for 97 is **1100001**

1.15.2.2 Fractions In Binary
        For the decimal number 25·125
        2 Tens + 5 Units + 1 Tenth + 2 Hundredths + 5 Thousandths

The Binary Number %111·111 Means:
1 Four + 1 Two + 1 Unit + 1 Half + 1 Quarter + 1 Eighth
Which is the same as 7·375
We use this method to convert Binary fractions into Decimal fractions.

1.15.2.3 Convertion of Binary Fractions into Decimal

Method 1:

Continue multiplying the fraction part by 2. If the doubled figure is greater than 1 then the next binary digit of the fraction is 1, else it is 0.
Example: Convert 0·625 into Binary

$0·625 × 2 = 1·25$
1 is the 1st digit right of the Point
$0·25 × 2 = 0·5$
0 is the 2nd digit right of the Point
$0·5 × 2 = 1·0$
1 is the 3rd digit right of the Point
$0·625 = \%0·101$

Method 2:

Subtract 2^{-n} where n increases by one. Where it is unsuccessful the nth digit right of the point becomes a 0, Otherwise it is a one.

Example: Convert 0·625 into Binary

$0·625 – 2^{-1}$ (i.e. 0·5) $= 0·125$
So the 1st digit after the Point is 1
$0·125 – 2^{-2}$ (i.e. 0·25)

Unsuccessful
The 2nd digit after the Point is 0
$0.125 - 2^{-3}$ (i.e. 0.125) = 0
The 3rd digit after the Point is 1
$0.625 = \%0.101$

1.15.3 Binary rules of Arithmetic

Rules of Binary Addition:
$0 + 0 = 0$
$0 + 1 = 1$
$1 + 0 = 1$
$1 + 1 = 0$
, and carry 1 to the next more significant bit

Examples:

1. $00011010 + 00001100 = 00100110$

1 1	Carries
0 0 0 1 1 0 1 0	= $26_{(base\ 10)}$
+ 0 0 0 0 1 1 0 0	= $12_{(base\ 10)}$
0 0 1 0 0 1 1 0	= $38_{(base\ 10)}$

2. $00010011 + 00111110 = 01010001$

1 1 1 1 1	CARRIES
0 0 0 1 0 0 1 1	= $19_{(base\ 10)}$
0 0 1 1 1 1 1 0	= $62_{(base\ 10)}$
0 1 0 1 0 0 0 1	= $81_{(base\ 10)}$

Rules of Binary Subtraction:
0 - 0 = 0
0 - 1 = 1, and borrow 1 from the next more significant bit
1 - 0 = 1
1 - 1 = 0

Examples:

1.   00100101 - 00010001 = 00010100

0	BORROWS
0 0 $\mathbf{\not{1}}$ ^{1}0 0 1 0 1	= $37_{(\text{base }10)}$
- 0 0 0 1 0 0 0 1	= $17_{(\text{base }10)}$
0 0 0 1 0 1 0 0	= $20_{(\text{base }10)}$

2.   00110011 - 00010110 = 00011101

0 ^{1}0 1	BORROWS
0 0 $\not{1}$ $\not{1}$ $\not{0}$ ^{1}0 1 1	= $51_{(\text{base }10)}$
- 0 0 0 1 0 1 1 0	= $22_{(\text{base }10)}$
0 0 0 1 1 1 0 1	= $29_{(\text{base }10)}$

Rules of Binary Multiplication:
0 * 0 = 0
0 * 1 = 0
1 * 0 = 0
1 * 1 = 1

Examples:

1. $00101001 * 000001100 = 11110110$

0 0 1 0 1 0 0 1	$=$ $41_{(base\ 10)}$
$\times$ 0 0 0 0 0 1 1 0	$=$ $6_{(base\ 10)}$
00 0 0 0 0 0 0 00 1 0 1 0 0 1 00 1 0 1 0 0 1	
0 0 1 1 1 1 0 1 1 0	$=$ $246_{(base\ 10)}$

2. $00101001 * 000001100 = 11110110$

0 0 0 1 0 1 1 1 1	$=$ $23_{(base\ 10)}$
$\times$ 0 0 0 0 0 0 1 1	$=$ $3_{(base\ 10)}$
1 1 1 1 1 0 0 0 1 0 1 1 1 0 0 0 1 0 1 1 1	
0 0 1 0 0 0 1 0 1	$=$ $69_{(base\ 10)}$

Binary Division:
Binary division is the repeated process of subtraction, just as in decimal division.
Example:
$00101011 * 00000110 = 00000111$
$42_{(base\ 10)} \ / \ 6_{(base\ 10)} \ = 7$

<u>1 1 1</u>	$= 7_{(base\ 10)}$
1 1 0| 00101010	$= 42_{(base\ 10)}$
<u>- 110</u>	$= 6_{(base\ 10)}$
1	borrows
-01	
<u>- 110</u>	
110	
<u>-110</u>	
0	

A negative number –n is most commonly represented in binary using the complement of the positive number n-1, so - 11=00001011 would be written as the complement of 10=00001010, or 11110101. This allows addition to be carried out with the usual carrying and the leftmost digit discarded, so 17-11 = 6 gives

```
00010001    17
11110101   -11
00000110     6
```

The number of times k that a given binary number b_n ... b_2 $b_1 b_0$ is divisible by 2 is given by the position of the first $b_k=1$ counting from the right. For example, 12 = 1100 is divisible by 2 twice, and 13 = 1101 is divisible by 2 zero times. The number of times that 1, 2, ... are divisible by 2 are 0, 1, 0, 2, 0, 1, 0, 3, 0, 1, 0, 2, 0, 1, 0, 4, 0, 1, 0, 2, ..., which is the binary carry sequence. The sequence a (n) given by the exponents of the highest power of 2 dividing n, i.e., the number of trailing 0s in the binary representation of n. For $n = 1, 2, ...$, the first few are 0, 1, 0, 2, 0, 1, 0, 3, 0, 1, 0, 2, ...

Real numbers can also be represented using binary notation by interpreting digits past the "decimal" point as negative powers of two, so the binary digits, ...b_2 $b_1 b_0$. b_{-1} b_{-2} ..., would represent the number

$$...+b_2.2^2 + b_1.2^1 + b_0.2^0 + b_{-1}.2^{-1} + b_{-2}.2^{-2} +...$$

Therefore, 1/2 would be represented as 0.1_2, 1/4 as 0.01_2, 3/4 as 0.11_2, and so on. The storage of binary numbers in computers is not entirely standardized. Because computers store information in 8-bit bytes (where a bit is a single binary digit), depending on the "word size" of the machine, numbers requiring more than 8 bits must be stored in multiple bytes.

Binary multiplication of single bit numbers (0 or 1) is equivalent to the AND operation, as can be seen in the following multiplication table.

x	0	1
0	0	0
1	0	1

1.15.4 Using Mathematica

An integer n may be represented in binary in *Mathematica* [5] using the command *BaseForm* [n, 2], and the first d digits of a real number x may be obtained in binary using *RealDigits*[x, 2, d]. Finally, a list of binary digits l can be converted to a decimal rational number or integer using *FromDigits* [l, 2]. The following table gives the binary equivalents of the decimal numbers from 1 to 30.

1	1	11	1011	21	10101
2	10	12	1100	22	10110
3	11	13	1101	23	10111
4	100	14	1110	24	11000
5	101	15	1111	25	11001
6	110	16	10000	26	11010
7	111	17	10001	27	11011
8	1000	18	10010	28	11100
9	1001	19	10011	29	11101
10	1010	20	10100	30	11110

1.16 Exercise 1

1.   Convert the decimal number 39 into binary arithmetic.

2.   Convert the decimal number 98 into binary arithmetic.

3.   Convert the binary number 10011 into decimal.

4.   Convert the decimal number 1.0 into binary arithmetic.

5.   Convert the decimal number 3.9 into binary arithmetic.

6.   Convert the decimal number 0.5 into binary arithmetic.

7.   Convert the decimal number 0.25 into binary arithmetic.

8.   Convert the decimal number 0.75 into binary arithmetic.

9.   Find primes from the following set of numbers;

     2 3 4 5 6 7 8 9 10 11 12 13 14 15.

10.   Evaluate $f(x) = \sqrt{1+x} - \sqrt{1-x}$ for x = 0.001

11.   a. Add the following binary numbers: 11110 + 11100.
       b. Compute 10001 - 110

12.   a. Multiply the following Binary numbers: 111 * 1010.
       b. Divide the following Binary numbers: 1110 / 111.

2 Boolean algebra.

2.1 Introduction

Boolean algebra was introduces by George Boole[6] to study logical operations. Boolean algebra, in addition to its applications in the field of logic, has two important applications. The first is the treatment of combination of sets of elements under the operations of intersection and union of sets. Secondly, with the idea of number of elements in a set, Boolean algebra becomes the foundation of the theory of probability.

Boolean algebra has played an important role in designing telephone switching circuits, automatic control devices, and electronic computers, which at present is the center of interest.

2.2 Elements and sets

We shall think of elements as basic objects, which form or constitute a Set. We shall use letters of alphabet in lower case to represent elements (a, b, c, x, y...) and capital letters to represent sets (A, B, X, Z ....). The number of elements of a set A, is called its *cardinality* and is denoted by $|A|$.

Two sets are important. One is the so-called Universal set (denoted by symbol 1), which consists of all elements under discussion, and referred to as the fundamental domain. Every set is a subset of the Universal set. The null set, has no elements and is denoted by 0.

In order to handle elements in algebra, we introduce the concept of a *unit set,* which is a set consisting of a single element. If x is an element then a *unit set,* is denoted by $\{x\}$.

The *complement* of a set X, is X', and is defined to be the set consisting of all elements of the *universal set,* which are not elements of X. As especial case, the *null* set, and the *universal* set are each complements of the other.

The following symbols are used to define the relation between sets.

$=$	X = Y the two Sets X, Y are equal
$\neq$	X $\neq$ Y the two Sets X, Y are unequal
$\subseteq$	X $\subseteq$ Y Set X is a subset of Set Y
$\not\subseteq$	X $\not\subseteq$ Y Set X is not a subset of Set Y

Examples:

-    If X = {1, 2, 3, 5}, Y = {1, 2, 3, 5}, Z = {1, 2, 3, 7},
     Then X = Y and X $\neq$ Z
-    If X = {1, 2, 3}, Y = {1, 2, 3}, Z = {1, 2, 3, 7},
     Then X is a subset of Z, X = Y and X $\neq$ Z

A Set X is defined as a **proper subset** of Set Y if X is a subset of Set Y, but is not equal to Y,

$$X \subseteq Y, X \neq Y.$$

Two sets are said to be **disjoint** if they have no elements in common.

Inclusion of Sets: X $\subseteq$ Y is called the inclusion relation.

Inclusion properties:

-    **Reflexivity:** A Set X is a subset of itself, X $\subseteq$ X
-    **Transitivity:** if X is a subset of Y and Y is a subset of Z, then X is a subset of Z. i.e.

X ⊆ Y and Y ⊆ Z implies X ⊆ Z.
- **Equality:** if X ⊆ Y and Y ⊆ X if and only if X = Y
- **Null Set:** the null Set is a subset of every other Set.

The following symbols are used to define the relation between elements and sets.

∈ m ∈ X means element m is a member of set X

⊆ X ⊆ Y means set X is a subset of set Y, i.e. X consists of entirely elements, which are members of set Y and set Y has one or more elements not in X, we say, X is a *proper subset* of Y.

= X=Y set X is identical to set Y, i.e. both sets have the same number of elements.

Examples of Sets:

- The following natural numbers form a Set N (8) 1,2,3,4,5,6,7,8, where the numbers 1 to 8, are the elements of the Set. Such Set is called a finite Set.
  If a Set has infinitely many members, then it is called infinite Set.
- The Set (N) of all natural numbers, is an infinite Set that Contains all natural numbers as its members.
- The Set (R) of all real numbers is an infinite Set that contains all real numbers as its members.
- The Set of real roots of the equation x2+1=0 is the Null Set 0, since there are no real roots to the equation.

2.3   The combination of sets

The notations most commonly used for combination of sets are as follows:

<u>Symbolic notations</u>   <u>Meaning</u>

X+Y, X ∪ Y, X v Y   Union of set X and set Y

XY, X ∩ Y, X ∧ Y   Intersection of set X and set Y

A', $\overline{A}$, ~A   Complement of set A

In order to illustrate these notations, ***Venn Diagrams*** are used.

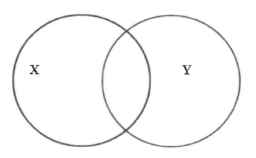

Fig 2-1

A Venn diagram for sets X & Y

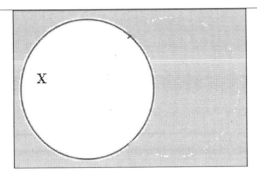

Fig 2-2

The complement of set X, X` is the shaded area.

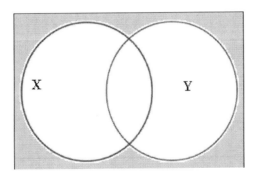

Fig 2-3

The complement of X + Y is X'Y'(shaded area.)

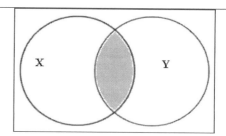

Fig 2-4

XY, X ∩ Y, X ∧ Y: Intersection of set X and set Y (shaded area)

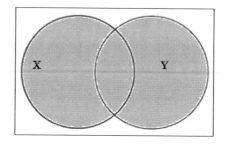

Fig 2-5

X + Y, X ∪ Y, X ∨ Y Union of set X and set Y (shaded area)

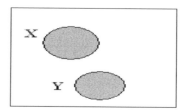

Fig 2-6

Fig 2-5 represents the union of two sets (shaded area). The two sets are not disjoint.

Fig 2-6 represents the union of two sets (shaded area). The two sets are disjoint.

2.4   Fundamental laws

If I and 0 denote the universal and the null sets respectively, the following are valid in algebra of sets for the arbitrary sets X, Y and Z. some of the laws reflect particular application, rather than Boolean algebra in general. Complementation suggests application to algebra of sets and tautology application to symbolic logic (see chapter 4.). Some of these laws do not apply to algebra of numbers, e.g. (6) to (10).

Commutative laws:	(1) $XY = YX$,
	(2) $X + Y = Y + X$
Associative laws:	(3) $X(YZ) = (XY)Z$,
	(4) $X + (Y + Z) = (X + Y) + Z$
Distributive laws:	(5) $X(Y + Z) = XY + XZ$,
	(6) $X + YZ = (X + Y)(X + Z)$
Tautology laws:	(7) $XX = X$,
	(8) $X + X = X$
Absorption laws:	(9) $X(X + Y) = X$,
	(10) $X + XY = X$

Complementation laws: (11) XX' = 0,
                             (12) X + X' = I
Double complementation law: (13) (X')'=X
De Morgan laws: (14) (XY)' = X' + Y',
                             (15) (X + Y)' = X'Y'

Operation with O and I:

   OX=O   IX=X   O' = I
   I +X = I   O+X=X   I' =O

Example 1:

   Expand (X + Y) (Z' + W) into a polynomial.

Solution:
   From the Commutative, Associative and   Distributive
   laws above We readily have:
   Z'X + Z'Y + WX + WY

Example 2:

   Determine a relation between I and 0

Solution:
   0 = I and   I = 0

Example 3:

   Prove A (B $\overline{C}$) = (AB) ($\overline{AC}$)

Solution:

Using the laws of set of algebra we have

$$(AB)\,(\overline{\overline{A}C}) = AB\,(\overline{A}+\overline{C}) \qquad \text{De Morgan}$$
$$= AB\,\overline{A} + AB\,\overline{C} \qquad \text{Distributive}$$
$$= A\,\overline{A}\,B + AB\,\overline{C} \qquad \text{Commutative}$$
$$= 0B + AB\,\overline{C} \qquad \text{Complement}$$
$$= AB\,\overline{C}$$

2.5   Definition of a Boolean Algebra

Given a class of elements C together with two binary operations (+) and (.), then this constitutes Boolean algebra if and only if the following postulates hold:

1.   The operations (+) and (.) are commutative.
2.   There exists in C distinct elements 0 and I such that
     $A.I = A$ $\qquad$ $A + 0 = A$ for every element in C
3.   Each operation is distributive over the other.
4.   For every element a in C there exists an element a` in C
     Such that
     $a + a` = I$ $\qquad$ a. a`=0

Any two symbols i.e. $\cup$ and $\cap$ which satisfy the postulates, would be a Boolean algebra.

Examples:

1.   For every element a in Boolean algebra C,
     $a + a = a$ $\quad$ and $aa = a$.

Proof: a = a + 0   by postulate 2
          = a + aa`   by postulate 4
          = (a + a) (a +a`)   by postulate 3
          = (a + a) (I)   by postulate 4
          = a + a   by postulate 2
2.   For every element a in Boolean algebra C,
          a + I = I   and a0 = 0
     Proof: I = a + a`   by postulate 4
              = a + a` (I)   by postulate 2
              = (a + a`) (a +I)   by postulate 3
              = I (a + I)   by postulate 4
              = a + I   by postulate 2

2.6   Transformation

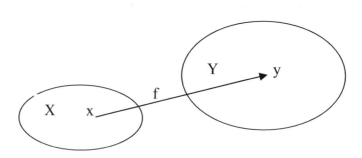

Fig 2-3

Transformation of f from set X to set Y
A transformation or a mapping f is referred to as a
function. In Fig 2-4, a mapping f assigns on element y ∈
Y an element x ∈ X,

$$y = f(x)$$

y is the image of x under the mapping f.

2.7   Exercise 2

1. A stack of books consists of Red, yellow and black books. All the red books and some of the black books are written in English. The remainder of the black books are written in Arabic. The yellow books are written in French. The set of all books in the stack is the universal set. The other sets are denoted as follows: R is the set of red books, Y is the set of yellow books, B is the set of black books, E is the set of books written in English, F is the set of books written in French and A is the set of books written in Arabic. Describe, in words, the following sets:

    i.   Y+A
    ii. RB`
    iii. A(B+R)
    iv. B+BR

2. Draw Venn diagram for the sets X, Y and Z. Shade the indicated area.
    i.   AC
    ii. A+BC
    iii. (A+B)(A+C)

3. Draw Venn diagram for each of the following. Shade the indicated area.
    i.   A+A`BC
    ii. (A+B`)(A`+C)

4. Expand (X+Y) (Z+W) into a polynomial.

5.   Factor the polynomial AC+AD+BC+BD into linear factors.

6.   Simplify $X(X`+Y)+ Y(Y+Z) + Y$

3   Probability
3.1   Definition

Probability is the branch of mathematics that studies the possible outcomes of given event and is a numerical measure of the likelihood of the event occurring. In common usage, the word "probability" is used to mean the chance that a particular event (or set of events) will occur expressed on a linear scale from 0 (impossibility) to 1 (certainty), also expressed as a percentage between 0 and 100%.

A properly normalized function that assigns a probability "density" to each possible outcome within some interval is called a probability function (or probability distribution function), and its cumulative value (integral for a continuous distribution or sum for a discrete distribution) is called a distribution function (or cumulative distribution function). The probability that a variate X assumes the element x is denoted **P(X=x)**.

3.2   Rules of probability

The two fundamental laws of probability are:
-    addition rule of probability
-    multiplication rule of probability

Addition rule:
Mutually exclusive events: If A and B are two mutually exclusive events, then the probability of obtaining either A or B is equal to the probability of obtaining A plus probability of obtaining B and written in the following form

$$\textbf{P (A or B)} = \textbf{P (A)} + \textbf{P (B)} \qquad (3.2.1)$$

Non-Mutually exclusive events: If A and B are non-mutually exclusive events, then A or B means that A occurs or B occurs or both A and B occur simultaneously. Therefore we have:

P (A or B) = P (A) + P (B)-P (A and B)   (3.2.2)

Thus, subtracting the joint occurrence of A and B to avoid double counting.

The two rules above can be represented by Venn diagram as follows:

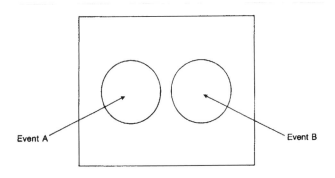

Mutually exclusive events

Fig. 3-1

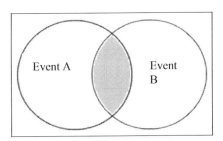

Non-mutually exclusive events

Fig. 3-2

In general for more than two events we have:

For Mutually exclusive events: P (A or B or C or …) = P(A) + P(B) + P(C) + …, and for Non- mutually exclusive events: P (A or B or C or …) = P(A) + P(B) + P(C) + …-P(A and B) -P(A and C) -P(B and C) +P(A and B and C) ….

The following Venn diagrams show the case of three events.

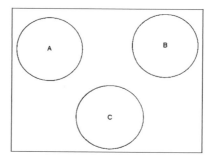

Fig. 3-3

Mutually exclusive events

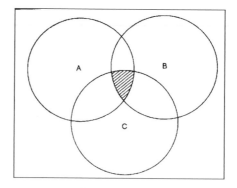

Fig. 3-4

Non-mutually exclusive events

Multiplication rule:

-       Dependent events:

P (A and B) = P (A) × P (B|A)   (3.2.3)
P (B|A) means probability of B occurring given that A has
already occurred.
-         Independent events:
P (A and B) = P (A) + P (B)   (3.2.4)

3.3   Join Probability

If in a random process, each outcome is equally likely to happen
and if the collection of all possible outcomes is S and the collection
of desired outcomes is A, the **probability** of A is given by:

$$P (A) = \text{Number of A/Number of S} = n (A)/n(S)$$

A is a subset of S, and therefore $0 \leq n (A) \leq n(S)$ and

$$0 \leq P (A) \leq 1$$

The probability of an unwanted outcome $\overline{A}$ is:

$$P(\overline{A}) = 1 - P(A)$$

Which may be computed as follows:

$$P(\overline{A}) = \frac{n(\overline{A})}{n(S)} = \frac{n(S) - n(A)}{n(S)} = 1 - \frac{n(A)}{n(S)} = 1 - P(A)$$

The probability of the desired outcomes is the sum of the
probability of each event resulting in a desired outcome. Suppose

that the set of desired outcomes A has M different events, i.e., A = (a_m | m= 1,2,3,…M). The Join Probability indicates that:

$$P(A) = n(A)/n(S)$$

$$= (n(a_1) + n(a_1) + \ldots n(a_M)) / n(S)$$

$$\sum_{m=1}^{M} P(a_m) = \frac{M}{n(S)}$$

3.4   Conditional Probability

Suppose that A and B are two sets of outcomes. The probability of B under the condition that A has happened, denoted by P (B\A), can be expressed as:

$$P(B \setminus A) = \frac{P(A \cap B)}{P(A)}$$

3.5   Independency

Suppose that A and B are two sets of outcomes. If the probability of B was not affected by whether A has happened or not, A and B are two **independent** sets of outcomes. Combining the conditional probability and independency, we have

$$P(B \setminus A) = \frac{P(A \cap B)}{P(A)} = P(B) \Rightarrow P(A \cap B) = P(A)P(B),$$

which shows that A has no effect and A and B are independent.

3.6 Density Function

A probability density function f(x) gives the probability of each possible outcome x.

3.7 Distribution Function

A probability distribution function F(x) gives the probability of all possible outcomes accumulated from the reference outcome (starting point) up to the current outcome x. The probability density function and the probability distribution function have the following relationship:

Discrete System: $\quad F(x_j) = \sum_{k \leq j} f(x_k)$

Continuous System: $\quad F(x) = \int_{-\infty}^{x} f(v)dv$

3.8 Mean Value

Mean Value, mean, or expectation, denoted by μ, is the likely outcome in an average sense. The average of all outcomes in a large-sample random sampling process is expected to be (close to) the mean value which is defined as:

Discrete System: $\mu = \sum_{j} x_j f(x_j)$

Continuous System: $\mu = \int\limits_{-\infty}^{\infty} xf(x)dx$

3.9   Variance

Variance denoted by σ^2 gives the spread of a distribution measured from the likely outcome μ. It is defined as:

Discrete System: $\sigma^2 = \sum\limits_{j}(x_j - \mu)^2 f(x_j)dx$

Continuous System: $\sigma^2 = \int\limits_{-\infty}^{\infty}(x - \mu)^2 f(x)dx$

3.10   Standard Deviation

Standard deviation, denoted by σ , is the positive square root of the variance. Both variance and standard deviation are used to describe the spread of a distribution.

Discrete System: $\sigma = \sqrt{\sum\limits_{j}(x_j - \mu)^2 f(x_j)dx}$

Continuous System: $\sigma = \sqrt{\int\limits_{-\infty}^{\infty}(x - \mu)^2 f(x)dx}$

3.11   Exercise 3

3.   Probability.

1.   Find the number of ways the set {1, 2, 3} can be partitioned.

2.   A class of students were asked about their book collection. The probability that a student owned Arabic books was 0.3. The probability that they owned English books was 0.25. However, if you would aske the students that owned the Arabic books, there was a probability of 0.55 that they would also own English books.
Find

a. The probability that a student, chosen at random, will have both books.

b. A student with the Arabic books will also have the English books.

c. A student has the English books, but not the Arabic books

d. A student has neither book.

3.   A Lottery has 45 balls of which you choose 6. In the draw 6 main balls are chosen and a seventh bonus ball. Given that all 45 balls are equally likely to be drawn, what is the probability of winning the 6 balls?
Find the probability of choosing 5 balls, plus the bonus ball.

4.   Two independent events, A and B have

$P(A) = 0.7$ and $P(A \cup B) = 0.9$

Find $P(B)$ and $P(A \cap B)$

5. A company has 100 employees, 20 of whom are females. There are 10 male directors and 5 female directors. If a staff member is selected at random to be made redundant, find the probability that the redundant person would be a female or a director.

4   Mathematical logic

Logic is engaged with the study and analysis of methods of reasoning. Symbolic logic referred to here is in general described as the study of logic which make an extensive use of symbols as we shall see later in this chapter. In discussing logic, we shall center on the concept of proposition or statement. Here we shall illustrate that the algebra of logic is another example of a Boolean algebra. Propositional calculus or algebra of logic (sometimes referred to as calculus of sentences or mere as proposition), is where tools of algebra are used to examine whether sentences are true or false.

4.1   Language and logic

The language, as traditionally known, in terms of written and spoken words, expresses thoughts and reasoning. However, with the advancement of science, in particular computers, the concept of language has been drastically broadened to include mathematical logic. A language consists of expression like sentences, terms and statements. Expressions are as models of entities.

Syntax of the language: is the structure of the expressions of a language.

Semantics of the language: is the meaning of a language.

4.2   Propositional logic

A statement which can be labelled True or False is called a proposition. The following statements are propositional:

- $2 < 3$ (True)
- 3 is a prime (True)
- $6 < 5$ (False)

On the other hand a statement containing a variable is not a proposition. For example the statement x < 5 is not a propositional, since it is not meaningful to say it is true or false. However if we replace x by its value, the sentence becomes a proposition. If a proposition can be split into sub-propositions, it is called compound, otherwise it is called simple. "My car is low in gas and I can not drive it a long distance" is a compound proposition and may be split into the following simple propositions:

- My car is low in gas.
- I can not drive my car a long distance.

Any logical statement which contains a finite number of logical variables can be analyzed using a table which lists all possible values of the variables. Such table is known as the "Truth table".

Definition: A **closed sentence** is an objective statement which is either true or false.

Each of the following sentences is a closed sentence
- Every triangle has three sides. (True)
- Khartoum is the capital of the Sudan. (True)
- No prime number is even. (False)

Each of the closed sentences above has a truth value of either true or false.

Definition: An **open sentence** is a statement which contains a variable and becomes either true or false depending on the value that replaces the variable.

The following sentences are open sentences.
- $y + 3 = 7$ (variable is y)
- He got high marks.   (Variable is He)
- $z - 4 = 11$ (variable is z).

If the variable in the first sentence is 4, then the sentence is True otherwise it is False. Similarly for the other two sentences. The truth value of each open sentence depends on what value is used to replace the variable in that sentence.

Definition: The **negation** of statement p is "not x." The negation of x is symbolized by "~x." The truth value of ~x is the opposite of the truth value of p.

Example 1: Construct a truth table for the negation of p.

Solution:

X	~X
T	F
F	T

We can also negate a negation. For example, the negation of ~x is ~ (~x) or x. This is illustrated in the example below.

Example 2: Construct a truth table for the negation of x, and for the negation of not x.

Solution:

X	~X	~ (~x)
T	F	T
F	T	F

4.2.1   Logical operators

We shall consider the following operators:
- AND
- OR
- NOT
- IMPLIES
- Equivalence

-      XOR

The **AND**, and **OR** operators combine two logical values, whereas the **NOT** operator negates a single logical value.
Combining Logical Expressions:
If both values joined by the **AND** operator are true, the combined expression is true (**T**), otherwise it is false (**F**). If

  $x = 1 < 2$
  $y = 2 > 4$

  the result x **AND** y is **F**

because, although x is true, y is false. "**AND**", or **conjunction** operator is a "**binary**" operator as it is an operator that takes two operands. It is traditionally represented using the following symbol: ∧
It has the following truth table:

x	y	x ∧ y
T	T	T
T	F	F
F	T	F
F	F	F

Notice that x AND y is only T if both x and y are T.

The **OR** (or **disjunction**) operator is also a binary operator, and is traditionally represented using the following symbol: ∨ , It has the following truth table:

x	y	x ∨ y
T	T	T
T	F	T
F	T	T
F	F	F

x ∨ y is true whenever either x is true, y is true or both x and y are true. If at least one of the values joined by the **OR** operator is true, the combined expression is true. If

$$x = 1 < 2$$
$$y = 2 > 4$$

x **OR** y is   **T**

because, although *y* is false, *x* is true. Here OR is applied in the nonexclusive sense, meaning that the proposition is true if at least one the propositions comprising it is true. OR may also be used in the exclusive sense (strict disjunction), meaning x OR y is true if either x or y is true and x OR y is false if x and y are both true, and false.

The **NOT** (or **negation** or **inversion**) operator is a "**unary**" operator: it takes just one operand, NOT is traditionally represented using ("~").

Not has the following truth table:

x	**~ x**
T	F
F	T

~ x is the negation of x.

IMPLIES is an implication operator and is a binary operator, and here we denote it by the symbol: ⇒ **IMPLIES** has the following truth table:

x	**y**	**x ⇒ y**
T	T	T
T	F	F
F	T	T
F	F	T

So x ⇒ y follows the following reasoning:

1.   A True premise (x) implies a True conclusion (y), therefore T ⇒ T is T;

2.   A True premise cannot imply a False conclusion, therefore T ⇒ F is F; and

3.   You can conclude anything from a false assumption, so F ⇒ anything is T.

EQUIVALENCE is a binary operator, and is traditionally notated by ⇔, or by ≡ (means `if and only if`). **EQUIVALENCE** has the following truth table:

x	y	x ≡ y
T	T	T
T	F	F
F	T	F
F	F	T

x ≡ y is T if x and y are the same (are equal).

The **XOR** (exclusive OR) operator is a binary operator. It is not usually considered as a separate operator since it is dependent of the operators we have considered so far. It is not often used in programming. For our purpose here we shall assign "**X**" as the symbol for the XOR.

x	y	x X y
T	T	F
T	F	T
F	T	T
F	F	F

For the operator XOR, the above truth table show that x X y is T if either x is T or y is T, but not both. XOR can be written in terms of ANDs, ORs and NOTs.

An Example of construction of a truth table:

Let x denote a proposition, say "a quadrilateral is a parallelogram" and let y denote another proposition "the diagonals of quadrilateral are bisected by their intersection points. Using logical operators we obtain the following compound proposition.

$$(x \Rightarrow y) \wedge (y \Rightarrow x),$$

Which means: if x, then y, and if y, then x.

In the first two columns of the truth table, we write all possible combinations of the values of x and y, the two elementary propositions. The 3rd column holds the value of the implication $(x \Rightarrow y)$, similarly in the 4th column we enter the values of $(y \Rightarrow x)$. In the 5th and last column we enter the values of the conjunction (AND) of the two values in the 3rd and 4th columns. The truth table is as follows:

x	y	$x \Rightarrow y$	$y \Rightarrow x$	$(x \Rightarrow y) \wedge (y \Rightarrow x)$.
T	T	T	T	T
T	F	F	T	F
F	T	T	F	F
F	F	T	T	T

4.2.2 Properties of Logical Operators.

Reference is made to Annex 1 listing axioms and properties in both logical and Boolean symbols.

1. Commutativity:
   We recall the commutative properties of addition and multiplication as follows:
   $$x + y = y + x$$
   $$x \times y = y \times x$$

We first construct a truth table illustrating the
commutative property of AND by identifying the sub-
expressions x AND y and y AND x:

x	y	x AND y	y AND x
T	T	T	T
T	F	F	F
F	T	F	F
F	F	F	F

x AND y is only T when both p and q are T (and likewise
for y AND x); the equality of the last two columns of the
truth table verify that AND full fill the law of
commutativity.
Similarly , the operator OR full fill the law of
commutativity as seen from the following truth table.

x	y	x OR y	y OR x
T	T	T	T
T	F	T	T
F	T	T	T
F	F	F	F

x OR y (as well as **y OR x**) is T unless both x and y are F,
as the last two columns indicate.

2.   Associativity:

Since addition and multiplication are both associative, then:
$$x + (y + z) = (x + y) + z$$

$$x \times (y \times z) = (x \times y) \times z$$

Now we find if AND and OR are associative and consequently the following relations are valid.

$$x \wedge (y \wedge z) = (x \wedge y) \wedge z$$
$$x \vee (y \vee z) = (x \vee y) \vee z$$

Since three variables are involved, our truth table must contain eight rows. Beginning by investigating the associativity of AND. identifying the sub-expressions $y \wedge z$ and $x \wedge y$ we construct the truth table as follows:

x	y	z	y ∧ z	x ∧ y	x ∧ (y ∧ z)	(x ∧ y) ∧ z
T	T	T	T	T	T	T
T	T	F	F	T	F	F
T	F	T	F	F	F	F
T	F	F	F	F	F	F
F	T	T	T	F	F	F
F	T	F	F	F	F	F
F	F	T	F	F	F	F
F	F	F	F	F	F	F

The last two columns of the table are equal, and therefore AND is associative.

For the associativity of OR , similarly we construct the truth table below. The last two columns of the table are equal, and therefore OR is associative.

x	y	z	y ∨ z	x ∨ y	x ∨ (y ∨ z)	(x ∨ y) ∨ z
T	T	T	T	T	T	T
T	T	F	T	T	T	T
T	F	T	T	T	T	T
T	F	F	F	T	T	T
F	T	T	T	T	T	T
F	T	F	T	T	T	T
F	F	T	T	F	T	T
F	F	F	F	F	F	F

3. Distribution:

In Algebra, multiplication distributes over addition:
i.e. $x \times (y + z) = x \times y + x \times z$
Here we see whether AND distributes over OR.
i.e. $x \wedge (y \vee z) = (x \wedge y) \vee (x \wedge z)$.
We construct a truth table for the logical values x, y and z
as well as for sub-expression $y \vee z$, $x \wedge y$ and $x \wedge z$.

x	y	z	y ∨ z	x ∧ y	x ∧ z	x ∧ (y ∨ z)	(x ∧ y) ∨ (x ∧ z)
T	T	T	T	T	T	T	T
T	T	F	T	T	F	T	T
T	F	T	T	F	T	T	T
T	F	F	F	F	F	F	F
F	T	T	T	F	F	F	F
F	T	F	T	F	F	F	F
F	F	T	T	F	F	F	F
F	F	F	F	F	F	F	F

The last two columns of the table are equal.

OR distributes over AND as follows:
$$x \vee (y \wedge z) = (x \vee y) \wedge (x \vee z)$$
The truth table verifying this fact is constructed as shown below.

p	q	z	y ∧ z	x ∨ q	x ∨ z	x ∨ (y ∧ z)	(x ∨ y) ∧ (x ∨ z)
T	T	T	T	T	T	T	T
T	T	F	F	T	T	T	T
T	F	T	F	T	T	T	T
T	F	F	F	T	T	T	T
F	T	T	T	T	T	T	T
F	T	F	F	T	F	F	F
F	F	T	F	F	T	F	F
F	F	F	F	F	F	F	F

The last two columns of the table are equal.

3.   Complement.

      a.   logical negation ($\sqcup$ F = T, $\sqcup$ T = F)

b.   either x is true or x is false (x ∨ ⊔ x=T)

c.   x cannot be both true and false (x ∧ ~x = F)

Statement b. is always true (a **tautology**).

Statement c. is a **contradiction** (never true).

5.   Identities.

a.   The identity x AND T = x
is formally analogous to the algebraic identity
x * 1 = x
Such an analogy is called "**isomorphism**",
meaning same ("iso") shape ("morph"). Many
of the logical properties are isomorphic to
algebraic properties.To analyze such logical
expression; we construct a truth table with
additional columns for each sub-expression:

x	T	x AND T
T	T	T
F	T	F

When x has the value T, x AND T is T and
when x has the value F, x AND T is F. i.e. x
AND T has the same values as x in all cases.
(Notice that the first and last columns are
identical).

b.   Boundedness identity.
Bounded identity has no algebraic analogy. An
example x | T = T
Its truth table is

x	T	x OR T
T	T	T
F	T	T

We see, OR with T is T.

c.   The identity x OR F = x
is isomorphic to the algebraic identity
x + 0 = x
Its truth table is

x	F	x OR F
T	F	T
F	F	F

The 1st and last columns are identical.

d.   The identity x AND F = F is **boundedness**
identity. It is isomorphic to the algebraic
identity x * 0 = 0 and has the truth table

x	F	x AND F
T	F	F
F	F	F

It illustrates that anything ANDed with F is F.

6.   Envolution

The involution property
~ ~x = x,
is isomorphic to the algebraic identity
- (-x) = x , and has the following truth table:

x	~x	~ ~x
T	F	T

F	T	F

7.   Reflexibility

An "operator" is reflexive if
x "operator " x for any x

8.   Symmetry

An operator "Operator" is symmetric if
x "Operator" y
is the same as
y "Operator" x

9.   Transitivity

An operator "Operator" is transitive if
x "Operator" y
and
y "Operator" z
imply that
x "Operator" z.

10.   Idempotence

The idempotence of an operator "O" is the
following:
x O x = x, for any x.
Both AND and OR operators are idempotent:
x AND x = x

x	x ∧ x
T	T

F	F

X OR x = x

x	x ∨ x
T	T
F	F

11.   Absorption

The absorption properties are
x ∨ (x ∧ y) = x

x	**y**	**x ∧ y**	**x ∨ (x ∧ y)**
T	T	T	T
T	F	F	T
F	T	F	F
F	F	F	F

and
x ∧ (x ∨ q) = x

x	**y**	**x ∨ y**	**x ∧ (x ∨ y)**
T	T	T	T
T	F	T	T
F	T	T	F
F	F	F	F

In both cases above, y is "absorbed" into x.

12.   DeMorgan's Laws

These are: ~(x ∨ y) = ~x ∧ ~y and
~(x ∧ y) = ~x ∨ ~y, which are isomorphic to the
following algebraic properties

$$(a + b)' = a' * b' \text{ and}$$
$$(a * b)' = a' + b'$$

4.2.3   Logic gates and circuits
(see Annex 2)

4.2.4   Propositional Formulas

In studying properties of propositions we represent them by expressions called *PROPOSITION FORMS or FORMULAS.* Formulas are built from PROPOSITIONAL VARIABLES, which represent simple propositions, and symbols representing LOGICAL CONNECTIVES such as AND, OR, NOT, etc. Here the letters $x, y, z, \ldots$ used to denote propositional variables and the symbols such as $\Rightarrow \wedge \vee \equiv \neg$ denote the standard logical connectives.

`I went to the club or I did not go to the club` is a Proposition.

$x \vee \neg x$ is called a Formula expressing the logical structure of the proposition above, where x is the simple proposition ` I went to the club.`

The term propositional logic also often refers to the formal language of propositional formulas.

Negation: We use the symbol $\neg$ or ~ to denote negation.

Formalization (syntax): If α is a formula, then $\neg\alpha$ is also a formula. We say that the second formula is the NEGATION of the first.

Meaning (semantics): If a proposition is true, then its negation is false. If it is false, then its negation is true.

Example:
Let us look at the proposition:
He went to school yesterday (x).
He did not go to school yesterday(~x).
At the formula level we express the connection via the following truth table:

x	~x
T	F
F	T

If x is true, then ~x is false.
If x is false, the ~x is true.

Conjunction:

the symbol ∧ to denote conjunction.
Syntax: If x and y are formulas, then x ∧ y is also a formula.

Semantics:

If x is true and y is true, then x ∧ y is true. In all other cases, x ∧ y is false.
Truth table:

x	y	x ∧ y
T	T	T
T	F	F
F	T	F
F	F	F

Example 1.:

1.   He went to the school.
2.   she went home.
3.   he went to the school AND She went home.

Let x and y abbreviate the first and second sentence, then the third is represented by the conjunction x ∧ y.
Inclusive Disjunction:
Using the symbol ∨ to denote (inclusive) disjunction.

Syntax: If x and y are formulas, then x ∨ y is also a formula.
Semantics: If x is true or y is true or both are true, then x ∨ y is true. If x and y are both false, then x ∨ y is false.
Truth table:

x	y	x ∨ y
T	T	T
T	F	T
F	T	T
F	F	F

Example 2.:

Exclusive Disjunction

1. He is industrous.
2. She is lazy.
3. He is industrous OR She is lazy.

Using the symbol ⊕ to denote exclusive disjunction we have:

Syntax: As in the previous example if x and y are formulas, then x ⊕ y is also a formula.

Semantics: An exclusive disjunction x ⊕ y is true if, and only if, one of x or y is true, but not both.

Truth table:

x	y	x ⊕ y
T	T	F
T	F	T

F	T	T
F	F	F

Evaluation of Formulas:

The semantics of logical connectives determines how propositional formulas are evaluated depending on the truth values assigned to variables.Each possible truth assignment or valuation for the variables of a formula yields a truth value. The different possibilities can be summarized in a truth table.

Example:

$x \wedge \sim y$ (read ``x and not y'') and the truth table is as follows:

x	y	$\sim y$	$x \wedge \sim y$
T	T	F	F
T	F	T	T
F	T	F	F
F	F	T	F

Note that it is usually necessary to evaluate all subformulas as indicated by the respective rows.

Truth Tables

A truth table for a formula lists all possible ``situations'' of truth or falsity, depending on the values assigned to the variables of the formula.

Example:

If x,y,z are propositions, say x OR y OR z, then the truth table would be:

x	y	z	x ∨ y ∨ z
T	T	T	T
T	T	F	T
T	F	T	T
T	F	F	T
F	T	T	T
F	T	F	T
F	F	T	T
F	F	F	F

Each row in the truth table corresponds to one possible situation of assigning truth values to *x, y* and z.

We can deduce the pattern of the truth table with n variables easily. *n*=1, there are two rows, for *n*=2, there are four rows, for *n*=3, there are eight rows, and so on. there are two choices (true or false) for each of *n* variables, so in general there are 2^n rows for n variables.

As in arithmatic Parentheses are needed, other wise the meaning of the formula is not clear. For example, the expression x ∧ y ∨ z can be interpreted in two different ways:
- if x is false , y is false and z is true,
  then x ∧ y is false(x ∧ y) ∨ z is true
- y ∨ z is true and x ∧ (y ∨ z) is false.

In arithmetic one often specifies a precedence among operators (e.g. multiplication ahead of plus) to eliminate the need for some parentheses in certain programming languages. The same can be done for the logical connectives, though if in doubt use parentheses. The logical operators follow "*operator precedence*" (an implicit ordering). If parentheses are not used, the operator precedence for logical operators is:

-   First do the NOTs;

- Then do the ANDs;
- Then the ORs and XORs, and finally
- do the IMPLIES and EQUIVALENCEs.

The properties of the logical connectives can also be exploited to simplify the notation. For instance, disjunction is Commutative, and Associative (see section 4.2.2).

4.2.5 Logical value

Logical values for true and false. A *logical value* has two values: **false** (ie zero integer value) or **true** (i.e. not zero integer value). By convention, true logical value will be integer value -1.

4.3 Computer logic

Logic circuits are used to perform all the internal operations of a computer. Logic circuit components are called 'gates' (see Annex 3).   Computer logic is based on a branch of mathematical logic called Boolean algebra (see previous chapter).

4.3.1 Binary numbers

 Computers are based on a binary (0 and 1) number system. Computers use 'bits', which are either 'off' or 'on'. Originally in computers these were small electro-magnets formed in the shape of small donuts wrapped with a wire. An electrical current was used to turn these magnets on (have a permanent magnetic field) or turned off (remove the magnetic field). Sensors could determine if the magnetic donut was on or off. Present computers use smaller domains made by laser expensive etching, and computers of the future may use atomic on–off switches. An alternative is analogue computing, which is also based on a few, but different physical/mathematical building blocks.

Now most computers use digital computing. Digital computing is based on binary logic, which uses on-off bits. The inventor of binary logic was George Boole[5], who wrote *The Laws of Thought*, a largely unsuccessful attempt to codify human logic. His ideas do work for computers, however. Boolean algebra forms the basis for computer programming.

In digital logic all information is expressed in terms of 1's and 0's. 'on' is 1. 'off' is 0.

Numbers can be expressed in binary.
     0000 = 0.
     0001 = 1.
     0010 = 2.
     0011 = 3.
     And so on.

Letters can also be expressed in binary. For example, one could use
     A = 00000000000000000000000001,
     B = 00000000000000000000000010,
     C = 00000000000000000000000100,

     .

     .

     Y = 01000000000000000000000000,
     Z = 10000000000000000000000000.

A combination of numbers and letters is called an *alpha-numeric* system, which is basic to most communication.

4.3.2   Truth values.

Computers employ a system of logic based on the idea that a proposition is either true or false. (More recently attempts have been made to develop fuzzy logic where ideas can be true, false or in between.) In the binary true-false system, a proposition x can be true (x = 1) or false (x = 0). For example, the proposition, x, that two plus two equals five is false (x=0), while the proposition, x, that two plus two equals four is true (x=1).

4.4   Exercise 4

1.   Define a closed sentence. Identify the following sentences:

1.   Every triangle has three sides.
2.   Khartoum is the capital of Sudan.

3.   No prime number is even.

2. Define an open sentence.
   Identify the following sentences:

   1. $x - 2 = 5$
   2. $y + 3 = 10$
   3. He passed all the exams.

3.   Identify the variables in the sentences in question 2.
         Assume a value for each variable and conclude whether
         the sentence becomes true or false.

4.   Define negation.
         If p represent the closed sentence `the number 8 is even`,
         what does ~p mean?

5.   Define a truth table.
         Construct a truth table for the negation of y.

6.   Define a conjunction. If p and q are two statements, what
         does $p \wedge q$ represents.

7.   Construct a truth table for two statements p and q and the
         conjunction `p and q`.

8.   If r represents the statement `the number x is odd` and s
         represents the statement `the number x is prime`, can you
         list all truth values for $r \wedge s$ in a truth table?

9. Construct a truth table for each of the following conjunctions.

  1. x and y
  2. ~x and y
  3. ~y and x

5   **Matrices**

An m x n matrix A is an ordered set of numbers
(Real or complex) a_{ij},

$$A = \begin{bmatrix} a_{11} & a_{12} & \cdots & a_{1n} \\ a_{21} & a_{22} & \cdots & a_{2n} \\ \cdots & \cdots & \cdots & \cdots \\ a_{m1} & a_{m2} & \cdots & a_{mn} \end{bmatrix}$$

written in m rows and n columns as shown above. A matrix is a
rectangular array of numbers and the numbers in the array are
called elements of the matrix. The coefficient matrix a_{ij} denotes
the element of matrix A in the ith row and jth column. We call A
an m by n matrix, and the m by n is referred to as the dimension
of the matrix.
The matrix A is called square matrix if m = n.
A single- row (or single-column) matrix is called a vector.

5.1   Matrix equality

Two matrices $A = [a_{ij}]_{mxn}$ and $B = [b_{ij}]_{mxn}$ are equal if and   only if
they are of the same dimension and if $a_{ij} = b_{ij}$

5.2   Matrix multiplication

5.2.1   General rule of matrix multiplication

Definition: if $A = [a_{ij}]_{mxn}$ and $B = [b_{ij}]_{mxn}$, then the product of A &
B is C, which is the m x p matrix defined by
$AB = C = [c_{ij}]_{mxn}$ Where

$$c_{ij} = \sum_{k=1}^{n} a_{ij} b_{kj}$$

The matrix product AB is defined only when the number of columns of A is equal to the numbers of rows of B, and A & B are said to be Conformable.

Example:

$$\begin{bmatrix} 1 & 3 \\ 2 & 2 \\ 3 & 1 \end{bmatrix} \begin{bmatrix} 1 & 2 & 3 \\ 3 & 2 & 1 \end{bmatrix} = \begin{bmatrix} 1(1)+3(3) & 1(2)+3(2) & 1(3)+3(1) \\ 2(1)+2(3) & 2(2)+2(2) & 2(3)+2(1) \\ 3(1)+1(3) & 3(2)+1(2) & 3(3)+1(1) \end{bmatrix} = \begin{bmatrix} 10 & 8 & 6 \\ 8 & 8 & 8 \\ 6 & 8 & 10 \end{bmatrix}$$

5.3   Matrix addition

Definition: if $A = [a_{ij}]_{mxn}$ and $B = [b_{ij}]_{mxn}$ and $C = [C_{ij}]_{mxn}$ then
$C=A+B \Leftrightarrow c_{ij} = a_{ij} + b_{ij}$
The sum C of two m x n matrices A and *B* is an m x n matrix whose ij-components are the sum of ij components in A and B. The sum of two matrices that are not of the same size (dimension) is not defined.
Example:

Given the following two matrices

$$A = \begin{bmatrix} 10 & 0 & 6 \\ 4 & 8 & 8 \\ 3 & 8 & 5 \end{bmatrix}, B = \begin{bmatrix} 1 & 8 & 6 \\ 3 & 2 & 3 \\ 6 & 2 & 1 \end{bmatrix}$$

Find the sum A + B
Solution:

$$A + B = \begin{bmatrix} 11 & 8 & 12 \\ 7 & 10 & 11 \\ 9 & 10 & 6 \end{bmatrix}$$

5.4   Matrix subtraction

Definition: if $A = [a_{ij}]_{mxn}$ and $B = [b_{ij}]_{mxn}$ and $C = [C_{ij}]_{mxn}$ then
$C = A - B \Leftrightarrow c_{ij} = a_{ij} - b_{ij}$

The difference C of two m x n matrices A and B is an m x n matrix whose ij-components are the difference of ij components in A and B. The difference of two matrices that are not of the same size (dimension) is not defined.

Example:

Given the following two matrices

$$A = \begin{bmatrix} 10 & 0 & 6 \\ 4 & 8 & 8 \\ 3 & 8 & 5 \end{bmatrix}, B = \begin{bmatrix} 1 & 8 & 6 \\ 3 & 2 & 3 \\ 6 & 2 & 1 \end{bmatrix}$$

Find the sum A - B

Solution:

$$A - B = \begin{bmatrix} 9 & -8 & 0 \\ 1 & 6 & 5 \\ -3 & 6 & 4 \end{bmatrix}$$

5.5   Multiplication of a matrix by scalar

Definition: if $A = [a_{ij}]_{mxn}$, α is any scalar and $B = [b_{ij}]_{mxn}$ then
$$B = \alpha A \iff b_{ij} = \alpha\, a_{ij}$$

Example 1:

Compute 3A and tA, where

$$A = \begin{bmatrix} 3 & 1 \\ 2 & -1 \end{bmatrix}$$

Solution:

$$3A = 3\begin{bmatrix} 3 & 1 \\ 2 & -1 \end{bmatrix} = \begin{bmatrix} 9 & 3 \\ 6 & -3 \end{bmatrix} \text{ and } tA = t\begin{bmatrix} 3 & 1 \\ 2 & -1 \end{bmatrix} = \begin{bmatrix} 3t & t \\ 2t & -t \end{bmatrix}$$

Example 2:

Using the matrices

$$A = \begin{bmatrix} 2 & 3 \\ 3 & 2 \\ 4 & 6 \end{bmatrix}, \; B = \begin{bmatrix} 3 & 6 & 4 \end{bmatrix}, \text{ find BA}$$

Solution:

$$BA = \begin{bmatrix} 3 & 6 & 4 \end{bmatrix}\begin{bmatrix} 2 & 3 \\ 3 & 2 \\ 4 & 6 \end{bmatrix}$$

$$= [(3\times2) + (6\times3) + (4\times4) \quad (3\times3) + (6\times2) + (4\times6)]$$

$$= [40 \quad 45]$$

Example 3:

Using the matrices

$$A = \begin{bmatrix} 2 & 3 & 4 \\ 5 & 6 & 7 \end{bmatrix}, B = \begin{bmatrix} 2 \\ 3 \\ 4 \end{bmatrix},$$

Compute AB.

Solution:

$$AB = \begin{bmatrix} 2 & 3 & 4 \\ 5 & 6 & 7 \end{bmatrix}\begin{bmatrix} 2 \\ 3 \\ 4 \end{bmatrix} = \begin{bmatrix} 2\times2+3\times3+4\times4 \\ 5\times2+6\times3+7\times4 \end{bmatrix} = \begin{bmatrix} 29 \\ 56 \end{bmatrix}$$

5.6   Zero matrixes

Definition:
If all elements of an m x n matrix are zero, then the matrix is called a zero matrix and is denoted by O or by O_{mXn}. If A is any m x n matrix, then   A+0=A=0+A

5.7   A scalar matrix S

A scalar matrix S is a diagonal matrix with all diagonal elements alike.
$a_{1,1} = a_{i,i}$ for (i = 1,2,3,..n)

5.8   A symmetric matrix

A square matrix is called symmetric if it is equal to its transpose.
Then $a_{i,j} = a_{j,i}$, for all i and j

5.9   A skew-symmetric matrix

A square matrix is called skew-symmetric if it is equal to the opposite of its transpose.

Then $a_{i,j} = -a_{j,i}$, for all i and j.

5.10   Negative of a matrix

Definition: The negative of a matrix A (-A) is the matrix whose elements are the negative of the corresponding elements of A. Negative of a matrix:

$$B = - A = (-1)A \Leftrightarrow b_{ij} = -a_{ij}$$

Example:

Compute A - B

$$\text{if} \quad A = \begin{bmatrix} 3 & 1 \\ 2 & 1 \end{bmatrix} \quad B = \begin{bmatrix} 1 & 2 \\ 3 & 5 \end{bmatrix}$$

Solution:

$$A - B = A + (-1)B = \begin{bmatrix} 3 & 1 \\ 2 & 1 \end{bmatrix} + \begin{bmatrix} -1 & -2 \\ -3 & -5 \end{bmatrix} = \begin{bmatrix} 2 & -1 \\ -1 & -4 \end{bmatrix}$$

5.11   Properties of basic matrix operations

The following are valid for any matrices A, B, C for which the indicated operations are defined and for any scalar α and β.

$A + B = B + A$	Additive commutativity	5.11.1
$A + (B + C) = (A + B) + C$	Additive associativity	5.11.2
$(AB)C = A (BC)$	Multiplicative associativity	5.11.3
$(\alpha \beta A) = \alpha (\beta A)$		5.11.4
$\alpha (AB) = (\alpha A) B = A (\alpha B)$		5.11.5
$A (B + C) = AB + AC$	Distributivity	5.11.6
$(A + B)C = AC + BC$		5.11.7

| α (A+B) = α A+ α B | 5.11.8 |
| $(\alpha + \beta)$A= α A+ β A | 5.11.9 |

5.12   The identity matrix

Definition: An n x n matrix A = [a_{ij}] , whose diagonal elements, a_{11} , a_{22}, ...,, a_{nn}, are all 1 and whose other elements are all 0, is called (I_n) identity matrix of n order.
I_n can be written as
I_n = [δ_{ij}]$_{nxn}$,where δ_{ij} is known as Kronecker delta and defined by

$$\partial_{ij} = \begin{cases} 1 & if \quad i = j \\ 0 & if \quad i \pm j \end{cases}$$

5.13   Non-singular matrix

The non-singular matrix must satisfy the following:
1.   The matrix must be square.
2.   No column of the matrix consists of only zeros.
3.   It is not possible to generate any row of the matrix from the other rows, using only elementary row operations.

5.14   Inverse of a matrix

Definition: If A is an n x n matrix and there exists an n x n matrix A^{-1} such that A A^{-1} = A^{-1}A=I_n, then A is called nonsingular (or invertible) and A^{-1} is the inverse of A.

For a 2 × 2 Matrix, $A = \begin{bmatrix} a & b \\ c & d \end{bmatrix}$,

Its inverse is =

$$A^{-1} = \frac{1}{|A|} \begin{bmatrix} d & -b \\ -c & a \end{bmatrix}$$

$$= \frac{1}{ad - bc} \begin{bmatrix} d & -b \\ -c & a \end{bmatrix}$$

For a 3 X 3 Matrix, $A = \begin{bmatrix} a_{11} & a_{12} & a_{13} \\ a_{21} & a_{22} & a_{23} \\ a_{31} & a_{32} & a_{33} \end{bmatrix}$

The matrix inverse is

$$A^{-1} = \frac{1}{|A|} \begin{bmatrix} \begin{vmatrix} a_{22} & a_{23} \\ a_{32} & a_{33} \end{vmatrix} & \begin{vmatrix} a_{13} & a_{12} \\ a_{33} & a_{32} \end{vmatrix} & \begin{vmatrix} a_{12} & a_{13} \\ a_{22} & a_{23} \end{vmatrix} \\ \begin{vmatrix} a_{23} & a_{21} \\ a_{33} & a_{31} \end{vmatrix} & \begin{vmatrix} a_{11} & a_{13} \\ a_{31} & a_{33} \end{vmatrix} & \begin{vmatrix} a_{13} & a_{11} \\ a_{23} & a_{21} \end{vmatrix} \\ \begin{vmatrix} a_{21} & a_{22} \\ a_{31} & a_{32} \end{vmatrix} & \begin{vmatrix} a_{12} & a_{11} \\ a_{32} & a_{31} \end{vmatrix} & \begin{vmatrix} a_{11} & a_{12} \\ a_{21} & a_{22} \end{vmatrix} \end{bmatrix}$$

A general n x n matrix can be inverted using methods such as the Gauss-Jordan elimination, or Gaussian elimination.(see chapter 6.).

The inverse of a product **AB** of matrices **A** and **B** can be expressed in terms of A^{-1} and B^{-1}. Let

$$C = AB$$

Then $B = A^{-1}AB = A^{-1}C$

and $A = ABB^{-1} = CB^{-1}$

Therefore, $C = AB = (CB^{-1})(A^{-1}C) = CB^{-1}A^{-1}C,$

so $CB^{-1}A^{-1} = I,$

Where I is the identity matrix, and

$$B^{-1}A^{-1} = C^{-1} = (AB)^{-1}$$

Example:

Show that matrices A & B below are, inverse to each other.

$$A = \begin{bmatrix} 1 & 1 \\ 2 & 3 \end{bmatrix} \quad B = \begin{bmatrix} 3 & -1 \\ -2 & 1 \end{bmatrix}$$

Solution:

$$AB = BA = \begin{bmatrix} 1 & 0 \\ 0 & 1 \end{bmatrix} = I$$

5.15   Elementary operation of a matrix

The following elementary operations are useful in solving system of linear equation as we shall see in chapter 6.

- Multiplying a row of a matrix by scalar (see section 5.5)
- Adding one row to another row.
- Exchanging two rows.

5.16 Transpose of a matrix

Definition: The transpose of an m x n matrix $A = [a_{ij}]_{mxn}$, denoted by A^T, is the n x m matrix $B = [b_{ij}]_{mxn}$, defined by $b_{ij} = a_{ji}$. It follows that the transpose is obtained by interchanging the rows and columns of A. Matrix A is called **symmetric** if $A^T = A$.

Example:

$$\text{Given A} = \begin{bmatrix} 3 & 1 & -3 & 4 & 7 \\ 4 & 5 & 6 & 8 & 9 \\ 1 & 2 & 5 & 8 & -2 \end{bmatrix},$$

$$A^T = \begin{bmatrix} 3 & 4 & 1 \\ 1 & 5 & 2 \\ -3 & 6 & 5 \\ 4 & 8 & 8 \\ 7 & 9 & -2 \end{bmatrix}.$$

5.16.1 Properties of transpose operation

$$(A+B)^T = A^T + B^T$$
$$(\alpha A)^T = \alpha A^T$$
$$(AB)^T = B^T A^T$$
$$(A^T)^T = A$$
$$(A^T)^{-1} = (A^{-1})^T \ \text{....... When A is nonsingular}$$

5.17 Special matrices

- A matrix $D = [d_{ij}]_{nxn}$ is called a **diagonal matrix** if all its nondiagonal elements are zeros, i.e. $d_{ij} = 0$ whenever i is not equal to j
- A Diagonal matrix $D = [d_i \delta_{ij}]$ of order n is called a **scalar matrix** if all its diagonal elements d_i are equal, i.e.
  $d_1 = d_2 = ... = d_n = \lambda$
  $D = \lambda I_n$
- A matrix is called **upper-triangular** if all elements below the diagonal, are zero.
- A matrix is called **lower-triangular** if all elements above the diagonal, are zero.

Properties of special matrices:

- The sum of two upper-triangular matrices is upper-triangular, and the sum of two lower-triangular matrices is lower- triangular.
- The product of two upper-triangular matrices is upper-triangular, and the product of two lower-triangular matrices is lower- triangular.

5.18 Exercise 5.1

1. Verify the following basic matrix operations:
   $A+B=B+A$ & $A(B+C) = AB + AC$

2. Verify that the following basic matrix operations,

   $(AB)C = A(BC)$ & $A(B+C) = AB + AC$

are valid for,

$$A= \begin{bmatrix} 1 & 2 \\ 3 & 4 \end{bmatrix} , B = \begin{bmatrix} 1 & -2 \\ 2 & 3 \end{bmatrix} , C = \begin{bmatrix} 1 & 1 \\ 2 & 0 \end{bmatrix}$$

3.   Verify the distributive property
$\alpha\,(A+B) = \alpha\,A + \alpha\,B$

4.   Verify the distributive property
$(\alpha + \beta)A = \alpha\,A + \beta\,A$

5.   Compute AB, BA, AC, CA, where

$$A = \begin{bmatrix} 1 & 2 & 2 \\ 3 & 1 & 1 \end{bmatrix}, B = \begin{bmatrix} 2 & 1 \\ 2 & 4 \end{bmatrix}, C = \begin{bmatrix} -1 & 2 \\ 1 & 3 \\ 0 & 1 \end{bmatrix}$$

6.   Verify that $AI_n = I_nA = A$

7.   Given

$$A= \begin{bmatrix} 1 & 2 \\ 3 & 4 \end{bmatrix} , \quad \text{find } A^{-1}$$

8.   Show that $I^T_n = I_n$

9.   Verify the property $(A + B)^T = A^T + B^T$

10.   Show that the product of two n x n matrices is a
      diagonal matrix and that the product is commutative.

11.   Show that $A + A^T$ is symmetric for any n x n matrix A.

5.19   Determinants

5.19.1 Determinant of square matrix

If we have a square matrix A, we associate with it a certain
number called its determinant, which is denoted by det A or |A|. if
det A # 0, then A is said to be nonsingular.
-       If $A = [a_{11}]$, then det $A = a_{11}$

- For a 2 x 2 matrix, we determine det A as follows:

$$A = \begin{bmatrix} a_{11} & a_{12} \\ a_{21} & a_{23} \end{bmatrix}$$

$$\det A = \begin{vmatrix} a_{11} & a_{12} \\ a_{21} & a_{23} \end{vmatrix} = a_{11}\, a_{23} - a_{12}\, a_{21}$$

Rule: (+)   (−)

$$a_{11} \diagdown a_{12}$$
$$a_{21} \quad a_{22}$$

Multiply the elements on the rightward arrow and then subtract the product of the elements on the leftward arrow.

- For a 3 x 3 matrix, we determine det A as follows:

$$A = \begin{bmatrix} a_{11} & a_{12} & a_{13} \\ a_{21} & a_{22} & a_{23} \\ a_{31} & a_{32} & a_{33} \end{bmatrix}$$

$$\det A = \begin{vmatrix} a_{11} & a_{12} & a_{13} \\ a_{21} & a_{22} & a_{23} \\ a_{31} & a_{32} & a_{33} \end{vmatrix} =$$

$$a_{11}\, a_{22}\, a_{33} + a_{12}\, a_{23}\, a_{31} + a_{13}\, a_{21}\, a_{32} - a_{13}\, a_{22}\, a_{31} - a_{11}\, a_{23}\, a_{32} - a_{12}\, a_{21}\, a_{33}$$

Rule: (+) (+) (+)   (−) (−) (−)

$$a_{11}\; a_{12}\; a_{13}\; a_{11}\; a_{12}$$
$$a_{21}\; a_{22}\; a_{23}\; a_{21}\; a_{22}$$
$$a_{31}\; a_{32}\; a_{33}\; a_{31}\; a_{32}$$

Form the pattern above, adding the first and second columns and summing the product of the elements on the rightward arrow and then subtract the product of the elements on the leftward arrow.

Note; for Matrices of higher order of more than 3 x 3, computing their det is rather complicated, using the above scheme. Other scheme will be considered below.

5.19.2 Cofactor expansion

- Cofactors definition

Let A= $[a_{ij}]$ be an n x n matrix, and let M_{ij} be an (n-1) x (n-1) obtained from A by deleting the ith row and the jth column. The det M_{ij} is called the minor of a_{ij}. The number A_{ij} is defined by $A_{ij}=$ $(-1)^{i+j}$ det M_{ij} is called the cofactor of a_{ij}. The sign $(-1)^{i+j}$ forms the pattern

$$\begin{bmatrix} + & - & . & . \\ - & + & . & . \\ + & - & . & . \\ . & . & . & . \end{bmatrix}$$

5.19.3 Minors.

The minor of an element in a determinant is a determinant of the next lower order, obtained by deleting the row and the column in which that element lies. A minor M_{ij} is formed by omitting the ith row and the jth column of amatrix.
Example:
     The minor of element c in the following determinant

$$\begin{vmatrix} a & b & c \\ d & e & f \\ g & h & i \end{vmatrix}$$

is found by striking out the first row and 3rd column as follows

$$\begin{vmatrix} \overset{\leftarrow}{a} & \overset{\leftarrow}{b} & \overset{\leftarrow}{c} \\ d & e & \overset{\leftarrow}{f} \\ g & h & \overset{\leftarrow}{i} \end{vmatrix} = \begin{vmatrix} d & e \\ g & h \end{vmatrix}$$

Example:

$$A = \begin{bmatrix} 1 & 4 & 2 \\ 0 & 1 & 2 \\ 1 & 2 & 3 \end{bmatrix}$$

The minor of a_{11} is

$$|M_{11}| = \begin{vmatrix} 1 & 4 & 2 \\ 0 & 1 & 2 \\ 1 & 2 & 3 \end{vmatrix} = \begin{vmatrix} 1 & 2 \\ 2 & 3 \end{vmatrix} = -1$$

The cofactor of a_{11} is, $A_{11} = (-1)^{1+1} |M_{11}| = -1$

The minor of a_{23} is

$$|M_{23}| = \begin{vmatrix} 1 & 4 & 2 \\ 0 & 1 & 2 \\ 1 & 2 & 3 \end{vmatrix} = \begin{vmatrix} 1 & 4 \\ 1 & 2 \end{vmatrix} = -2$$

The cofactor of a_{23} is, $A_{11} = (-1)^{2+3} |M_{23}| = -2$

Theorem: If A is an n x n matrix and A_{ik} denotes the cofactor of a_{ik}, then det A can be expressed as a cofactor expansion using any row or column of A by the following formulas:

Det A $= a_{i1} A_{i1} + a_{i2}A_{i2} + \ldots + a_{in}A_{in} = \sum a_{ik}A_{ik}$ (5.19.1)

For $i = 1,2,\ldots\ldots$ n

Det A $= a_{1j} A_{1j} + a_{2j}A_{2j} + \ldots + a_{nj}A_{nj} = \sum a_{kj}A_{kj}$ (5.19.2)

For $j = 1,2,\ldots.,$ n

Formula (6.12.1) is the cofactor expansion or Laplace expansion of det A along the ith row, and Formula (2) is the cofactor expansion or Laplace expansion of det A along the jth column.

Example:

Compute det A   where

$$A = \begin{bmatrix} 1 & 4 & 2 \\ 0 & 1 & 2 \\ 1 & 2 & 3 \end{bmatrix}$$

Solution:

$$\det A = \begin{vmatrix} 1 & 4 & 2 \\ 0 & 1 & 2 \\ 1 & 2 & 3 \end{vmatrix} = 3+8+0-2-4-0=5$$

5.20 Properties of Determinants

- Property 1

The determinant of a matrix A is unchanged if any row or column is replaced by the sum of that row or column.

If Det $A = \begin{vmatrix} a_1 & b_1 \\ a_2 & b_2 \end{vmatrix}$, replacing 1st column by its sum, we have

$$\begin{vmatrix} a_1 + b_1 & b_1 \\ a_2 + b_2 & b_2 \end{vmatrix} = a_1b_2 + b_2b_1 - a_2b_1 - b_2b_1 = a_1b_2 - a_2b_1$$

$$= \text{Det } A$$

- Property 2

The determinant of a matrix A is multiplied by a constant k if any row or column is multiplied by k.

Example:

$$\begin{vmatrix} ka_1 & b_1 \\ ka_2 & b_2 \end{vmatrix} = k(a_1b_2) - k(b_1a_2) = k \begin{vmatrix} a_1 & b_1 \\ a_2 & b_2 \end{vmatrix}$$

$$= k(\text{Det. } A)$$

- Property 3

The determinant of the identity matrix I_n is 1.

- Property 4

The determinant of a matrix A is unchanged if a multiple of one row or column is added to or subtracted from another row or column. (Derived from 1 & 2).

Given det A $= \begin{vmatrix} a_1 & b_1 \\ a_2 & b_2 \end{vmatrix}$, we have

$\begin{vmatrix} a_1 + kb_1 & b_1 \\ a_2 + kb_2 & b_2 \end{vmatrix} = b_2(a_1 + kb_1) - b_1(a_2 + kb_2)$

$= b_2 a_1 + k\ b_2 b_1 - b_1 a_2 - k\ b_1 b_2$

$= b_2 a_1 - b_1 a_2 = \text{Det A}$

- Property 5
The determinant of a matrix A changes sign when two rows or columns are interchanged. (Derived from 1 & 4)

Example:

$\text{Det.A} = \begin{vmatrix} a_1 & b_1 \\ a_2 & b_2 \end{vmatrix} = a_1 b_2 - b_1 a_2 = -(b_1 a_2 - a_1 b_2)$

$= - \begin{vmatrix} b_1 & a_1 \\ b_2 & a_2 \end{vmatrix}$

- Property 6
If A has a zero in a row or column, then det A = 0 (follows from 2 for k = 0)

- Property 7
If any two rows or columns of A are equal or proportional, then det A = 0 (follows from 5)

- Property 8
If A is triangular, then det A is the product of the diagonal entries, i.e. det A = $a_{11}\ aa_{22}...a_{nn}$.

5.21 Multiplicative property of Determinants.

If A & B are n x n matrices, then Det (AB) = (det A) (det B)

5.22 Determinants and the inverse of a matrix

- Adjugate (classic adjoint) of a matrix
Definition: Let A = [a_{ij}] be an n x n matrix and let A_{ij} be the cofactor of a_{ij}. The cofactor matrix of A, denoted by Cof A, is defined as the n x n matrix whose ijth entry is A_{ij}a, that is
Cof A = [A_{ij}]n x n
The transpose of the cofactor matrix A is called the Adjugate of A denoted by adj.
Adj A = [A_{ij}]^T
- Inverse of a matrix
If A is an n x n matrix and nonsingular, then
A^{-1} = (1/det A) adj A

5.23 Exercise 5.2

1. Find the Determinant of

$$A = \begin{bmatrix} 1 & 4 & 2 \\ 0 & 1 & 2 \\ 1 & 2 & 3 \end{bmatrix}$$

2. If

$$A = \begin{bmatrix} a & b \\ c & d \end{bmatrix}, B = \begin{bmatrix} a+c & b+d \\ c & d \end{bmatrix}$$

Show that det A = det B

3. If

$$A = \begin{bmatrix} a & b \\ c & d \end{bmatrix}, B = \begin{bmatrix} a & b \\ kc & kd \end{bmatrix}$$

Show that det B = k(det A)

4. Compute det I_2

5. Find the value of the determinant

$$\begin{bmatrix} 3 & 0 & 2 \\ 1 & 4 & 3 \\ 2 & 1 & 2 \end{bmatrix}$$

6   Linear Algebra.

6.1   Linear equation

A linear equation in n unknowns is an equation of the form
$a_1x_1 + a_2x_2 + .., + a_nx_n = b$, where a_1 a_2 ...... a_n and b are
constant and the x_i's are the unknowns. The x_i's are called variables
with coefficients a_k.

The solution of such linear equation is an n numbers s_i such that
$a_1s_1 + a_2s_2 + ... + a_ns_n = b$

Example:

Find the solution of the linear equation: $2x_1 + 3x_2 = 8$

Solution: $x_1 = 4 - 3x_2/2$
Let $x_1 = t$ where t is an arbitrary number, then we get

$x_2 = (4 - t)2/3$

6.2   System of linear equations

A linear system of equations is a set of *n* linear equations in *k*
variables. Linear systems can be represented in matrix form as the
matrix equation

$$\mathbf{A}x = \mathbf{b} \tag{6.1}$$

The n unknowns, can be written **as an n-vector**

$$x = \begin{bmatrix} x_1 \\ x_2 \\ . \\ x_n \end{bmatrix} \tag{6.2}$$

The numbers on the right side can be written as **m-vector**

$$b = \begin{bmatrix} b_1 \\ b_2 \\ . \\ b_n \end{bmatrix} \qquad (6.3)$$

The coefficients are written as a rectangular array with m rows and n columns and A below is called the **coefficient matrix.**

$$A = \begin{bmatrix} a_{11} & a_{12} & \cdots & a_{1n} \\ a_{21} & a_{22} & \cdots & a_{2n} \\ \cdots & \cdots & \cdots & \cdots \\ a_{m1} & a_{m2} & \cdots & a_{mn} \end{bmatrix} \qquad (6.4)$$

Where **A** is the matrix of coefficients, **x** is the column vector of variables, and **b** is the column vector of solutions.

If $k < n$, then the system is (in general) over determined and there is no solution.

If $k = n$ and the matrix A is non-singular, then the system has a unique solution in the n variables. In particular, as shown by Cramer's rule, there is a unique solution if **A** has a matrix inverse A^{-1}. In this case,

$$x = A^{-1} b \qquad (6.5)$$

If **B**=**0**, then the solution is simply **x**=**0**.

6.3   Gaussian Elimination

Gaussian elimination is a method for solving matrix equations of the form

$$\mathbf{A}\,x = \mathbf{b} \tag{6.7}$$

To perform Gaussian elimination starting with the system of equations

$$
\begin{bmatrix}
a_{11} & a_{12} & \cdot & \cdot & \cdot & a_{1k} \\
a_{21} & a_{22} & \cdot & \cdot & \cdot & a_{2k} \\
\cdot & \cdot & \cdot & \cdot & \cdot & \cdot \\
\cdot & \cdot & \cdot & \cdot & \cdot & \cdot \\
\cdot & \cdot & \cdot & \cdot & \cdot & \cdot \\
a_{k1} & a_{k2} & & & & a_{kk}
\end{bmatrix}
\begin{bmatrix}
x_1 \\ x_2 \\ \\ \\ \\ x_k
\end{bmatrix}
=
\begin{bmatrix}
b_1 \\ b_2 \\ \\ \\ \\ b_k
\end{bmatrix}
\tag{6.8}
$$

The augmented matrix is formed by taking the matrix of coefficients and "augmenting it" by appending a column containing the numbers on the right side of the equations. The "augmented matrix equation" would be,

$$
\begin{bmatrix}
a_{11} & a_{12} & \cdot & \cdot & \cdot & a_{1k} & b_1 \\
a_{21} & a_{22} & \cdot & \cdot & \cdot & a_{2k} & b_2 \\
\cdot & \cdot & \cdot & \cdot & \cdot & \cdot & \\
\cdot & \cdot & \cdot & \cdot & \cdot & \cdot & \\
\cdot & \cdot & \cdot & \cdot & \cdot & \cdot & \\
a_{k1} & a_{k2} & & & & a_{kk} & b_k
\end{bmatrix}
\begin{bmatrix}
x_1 \\ x_2 \\ \\ \\ \\ x_k
\end{bmatrix}
\qquad (6.9)
$$

Here, the column vector in the variables **x** is carried along for labelling the matrix rows. Now, perform elementary row operations to put the augmented matrix into the upper triangular form

$$
\begin{bmatrix}
a'_{11} & a'_{12} & \cdot & \cdot & \cdot & a'_{1k} & b'_1 \\
0 & a'_{22} & \cdot & \cdot & \cdot & a'_{2k} & b'_2 \\
\cdot & \cdot & \cdot & \cdot & \cdot & \cdot & \\
\cdot & \cdot & \cdot & \cdot & \cdot & \cdot & \\
\cdot & \cdot & \cdot & \cdot & \cdot & \cdot & \\
0 & 0 & & & & a'_{kk} & b'_k
\end{bmatrix}
\qquad (6.10)
$$

Solve the equation of the kth row for x_k, then substitute back into the equation of the (k-1) st row to obtain a solution for x_{k-1}, etc., using the formula

$$
x_i = \frac{1}{a'_{ii}} \left(b'_i - \sum_{j=i+1}^{k} a'_{ij} x_j \right)
\qquad (6.11)
$$

Examples:

1.   Consider the matrix equation

$$\begin{bmatrix} 9 & 3 & 4 \\ 4 & 3 & 4 \\ 1 & 1 & 1 \end{bmatrix} \begin{bmatrix} x_1 \\ x_2 \\ x_3 \end{bmatrix} = \begin{bmatrix} 7 \\ 8 \\ 3 \end{bmatrix}$$

The augmented form, would be,

$$\begin{bmatrix} 9 & 3 & 4 & 7 \\ 4 & 3 & 4 & 8 \\ 1 & 1 & 1 & 3 \end{bmatrix} \begin{bmatrix} x_1 \\ x_2 \\ x_3 \end{bmatrix}$$

Switching the first and third rows gives

$$\begin{bmatrix} 1 & 1 & 1 & 3 \\ 4 & 3 & 4 & 8 \\ 9 & 3 & 4 & 7 \end{bmatrix} \begin{bmatrix} x_1 \\ x_2 \\ x_3 \end{bmatrix}$$

Subtracting 9 times the first row from the third row gives

$$\begin{bmatrix} 1 & 1 & 1 & 3 \\ 4 & 3 & 4 & 8 \\ 0 & -6 & -5 & -20 \end{bmatrix} \begin{bmatrix} x_1 \\ x_2 \\ x_3 \end{bmatrix}$$

Subtracting 4 times the first row from the second row gives

$$\begin{bmatrix} 1 & 1 & 1 & 3 \\ 0 & -1 & 0 & -4 \\ 0 & -6 & -5 & -20 \end{bmatrix}\begin{bmatrix} x_1 \\ x_2 \\ x_3 \end{bmatrix}$$

Finally, adding -6 times the second row to the third row gives

$$\begin{bmatrix} 1 & 1 & 1 & 3 \\ 0 & -1 & 0 & -4 \\ 0 & 0 & -5 & 4 \end{bmatrix}\begin{bmatrix} x_1 \\ x_2 \\ x_3 \end{bmatrix}$$

Restoring the transformed matrix equation gives

$$\begin{bmatrix} 1 & 1 & 1 \\ 0 & -1 & 0 \\ 0 & 0 & -5 \end{bmatrix}\begin{bmatrix} x_1 \\ x_2 \\ x_3 \end{bmatrix} = \begin{bmatrix} 3 \\ -4 \\ 4 \end{bmatrix},$$

Solving we get, $x_3 = -4/5$, $x_2 = 4$, and then back-substituting to find $x_1 = -1/5$.

2.   Solve the system of linear equations.

$$2x_1 + 4x_2 + 8x_3 = 16$$
$$x_1 + x_2 + x_3 = 1$$
$$x_1 + 3x_2 + x_3 = 2$$

Solution: First, we write the augmented matrix for this system.

$$\begin{pmatrix} 2 & 4 & 8 & | & 14 \\ 1 & 1 & 1 & | & 3 \\ 1 & 3 & 1 & | & 5 \end{pmatrix}$$

After dividing each element in the first row by 2 we get the following matrix.

$$\begin{pmatrix} 1 & 2 & 4 & | & 7 \\ 1 & 1 & 1 & | & 3 \\ 1 & 3 & 1 & | & 5 \end{pmatrix}$$

Now we replace the second and the first row by their sums with the first row multiplied by -1. That leads to the matrix.

$$\begin{pmatrix} 1 & 2 & 4 & | & 7 \\ 0 & -1 & -3 & | & -4 \\ 0 & 1 & -3 & | & -2 \end{pmatrix}$$

After replacing the third row by its sum with the second row the Gaussian Elimination Procedure is completed.

$$\begin{pmatrix} 1 & 2 & 4 & | & 7 \\ 0 & -1 & -3 & | & -4 \\ 0 & 0 & -6 & | & -6 \end{pmatrix}$$

We can put back variables x_1, x_2, x_3 and solve the system "backwards" starting from the last equation.

$$x_1 + 2x_2 + 4x_3 = 7$$
$$-x_2 - 3x_3 = -4$$
$$-6x_3 = -6$$

The system has the only solution: $x_1 = x_2 = x_3 = 1$

3.   Solve the system of linear equations.

$$2x_1 + 4x_2 + 8x_3 = 8$$
$$x_1 + x_2 + x_3 = 3$$
$$2x_2 + 6x_3 = 2$$

Solution: First, we write the augmented matrix for this system.

$$\begin{pmatrix} 2 & 4 & 8 & | & 8 \\ 1 & 1 & 1 & | & 3 \\ 0 & 2 & 6 & | & 2 \end{pmatrix}$$

After dividing each element in the first row by 2 we get the following matrix.

$$\begin{pmatrix} 1 & 2 & 4 & | & 4 \\ 1 & 1 & 1 & | & 3 \\ 0 & 2 & 6 & | & 2 \end{pmatrix}$$

We replace the second row by its sum with the first row multiplied by "-1".

$$\begin{pmatrix} 1 & 2 & 4 & | & 4 \\ 0 & -1 & -3 & | & -1 \\ 0 & 2 & 6 & | & 2 \end{pmatrix}$$

After replacing the third row by its sum with the second row multiplied by "2" we get the matrix.

$$\begin{pmatrix} 1 & 2 & 4 & | & 4 \\ 0 & -1 & -3 & | & -1 \\ 0 & 0 & 0 & | & 0 \end{pmatrix}$$

We reduce the original system to the following form.
$$x_1 + 2x_2 + 4x_3 = 4$$
$$-x_2 - 3x_3 = -1$$

This system has infinitely many solutions. Indeed, the variable x_3 can take any real value. Mathematical representation of this fact looks as follows.
$$x_3 = t, \text{ where t can take any number.}$$

Now the second equation of our system implies that
$$x_2 = 1 - 3t$$
Finally, the first equation gives us.
$$x_1 = 2 + 2t$$

The system has infinitely many solutions. t is an arbitrary number. This is the general solution of the system.

4.   Solve the system of linear equations.
$$2x_1 + 4x_2 + 8x_3 = 8$$
$$x_1 + x_2 + x_3 = 3$$
$$2x_2 + 6x_3 = 1$$

Solution: This is an example of **inconsistent** system. First, we write the augmented matrix for this system.

$$\begin{pmatrix} 2 & 4 & 8 & | & 8 \\ 1 & 1 & 1 & | & 3 \\ 0 & 2 & 6 & | & 1 \end{pmatrix}$$

Follow the same steps as in the previous two examples; we obtain the following augmented matrix.

$$\begin{pmatrix} 1 & 2 & 4 & | & 4 \\ 0 & -1 & -3 & | & -1 \\ 0 & 0 & 0 & | & -1 \end{pmatrix}$$

According to the last line of the augmented matrix -1 is equal to 0 which is wrong, and that means the system does not have any solutions. Such systems are called **inconsistent**.

We conclude that any linear system falls in one of the following categories.

- The system has the only solution.
- The system has infinitely many solutions.
- The system is inconsistent. That means it does not have any solutions.

6.4   System of linear equations and Cramer's Rule

As shown in (6.1) a system of n equations in n unknowns can be expressed in matrix form as

$$Ax = b$$

If A is nonsingular, then the system has a unique solution given by

$$x = A^{-1} b$$

$$x = A^{-1} b = (1/\det A)(\text{adj } A)b$$

Cramer's rule:

Theorem (Cramer rule): If $Ax = b$, the system of n linear equations in n unknowns such that det A # 0, then the system has a unique solution

$$x = \begin{bmatrix} x_1 \\ x_2 \\ . \\ . \\ x_n \end{bmatrix}$$

given by :

$$x_1 = \det A_1 / \det A, \ x_2 = \det A_2 / \det A, \ \ldots\ldots, x_n = \det A_n / \det A$$

Consider the following system of equations:

$$6x_1 + 3x_2 + 3x_3 = 9$$
$$x_1 - x_2 - x_3 = 0$$
$$2x_1 + 4x_2 + 2x_3 = 0$$

$$D = \begin{vmatrix} 6 & 3 & 3 \\ 1 & -1 & -1 \\ 2 & 4 & 2 \end{vmatrix} = 18$$

$$D\,x_1 = \begin{vmatrix} 9 & 3 & 3 \\ 0 & -1 & -1 \\ 0 & 4 & 2 \end{vmatrix} = 18$$

$$D x_2 = \begin{vmatrix} 6 & 9 & 3 \\ 1 & 0 & -1 \\ 2 & 0 & 2 \end{vmatrix} = -36$$

$$D x_3 = \begin{vmatrix} 6 & 3 & 9 \\ 1 & -1 & 0 \\ 2 & 4 & 0 \end{vmatrix} = 54$$

$x_1 = D x_1 / D = 18/18 = 1$

$x_2 = D x_2 / D = -36/18 = -2$

$x_3 = D x_3 / D = 54/18 = 3$

6.5   Exercise 6

2.   Find the solution of set of

a) $2x_1 - x_2 = 1$

b) $2x_1 + x_2 - x_3 = 2$

2.   Find the solution of the following system of equations

$3x_1 - 2x_2 = 12$

$2x_1 - 5x_2 = 11$

3.   Find the solution of the following system of equations

$x_1 - x_2 = 3$

$2x_1 + 3x_2 = 2$

$3x_1 + 2x_2 = 5$

4.   Write the systems of problem 2 and 3 in matrix form

5.   Use Cramer's rule to solve

$3x_1 + x_2 = 10$

$2x_1 - x_2 = 5$

7   Vectors

Graphically, a vector is represented by an arrow, defining the direction, and the length of the arrow defines the vector's magnitude. If we denote one end of the arrow by the origin O and the tip of the arrow by Q. Then the vector V may be represented algebraically by OQ.

7.1   Geometric vectors

1. Definitions: A vector is a quantity characterized by magnitude and direction. The vector v has a direction from P to Q. P is called the initial point and Q is the terminal point. The length PQ is the magnitude of the vector, and is denoted by v.

Two vectors are equal, if they have the same magnitude and direction.

2. Addition of vectors:

Triangle rule   parallelogram law

3. Zero vectors (0):

A zero vector is a vector that has magnitude 0 and any direction.

4.   Negative vector:

If v is a nonzero vector, then -v is the negative of v, and has the same magnitude as v and direction opposite of v. The negative vector has the following property.

$$v + (-v) = 0$$

5.   Scalar (real number) multiplication:

Any quantity which has a magnitude but no direction associated with it is called a **"scalar"** **e.g.** speed, mass and temperature.
The product of a scalar, α say, times a vector V, is another vector, which has the same direction as **V** but with a different magnitude.

The scalar multiplication of a vector is defined to be a vector αv whose magnitude is
$$\alpha v = |\alpha| v.$$

7.2   Analytical representation of vectors

- Vector in 2-space

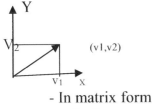

- In matrix form

$$v = \begin{bmatrix} v_1 \\ v_2 \end{bmatrix}$$

v_1 and v_2 are the components of v relative to the given coordinate System and they are real numbers.
Using matrix operations, we get the following vector operations:

- Equality of vectors: If

$$v = \begin{bmatrix} v_1 \\ v_2 \end{bmatrix} \quad u = \begin{bmatrix} u_1 \\ u_2 \end{bmatrix}$$

Then, $u = v \iff u_1 = v_1,\ u_2 = v_2$ (7.2.1)

- Vector addition:

$$v+u = \begin{bmatrix} v_1 + u_1 \\ v_2 + u_2 \end{bmatrix}$$ (7.2.2)

- Zero vectors:

$$0 = \begin{bmatrix} 0 \\ 0 \end{bmatrix}$$ (7.2.3)

- Scalar multiplication:

$$\alpha \, v = \begin{bmatrix} \alpha v_1 \\ \alpha v_2 \end{bmatrix} \qquad\qquad (7.2.4)$$

- Negative of v:

$$-v = \begin{bmatrix} -v_1 \\ -v_2 \end{bmatrix} \qquad\qquad (7.2.5)$$

7.3   Cartesian n-Space

Definition: A point in n-space can be represented by real numbers, $(x_1, x_2, ..., x_n)$, where $x_1, x_2, ..., x_n$ are the coordinates of the point. Thus a vector in n-space can be represented by n x 1 matrix

$$v = \begin{bmatrix} v_1 \\ v_2 \\ .. \\ .. \\ v_n \end{bmatrix} \qquad\qquad (7.2.6)$$

7.4   Exercise 7

1.   Define a Vector.

2.   Define a Scalar quantity.

3.   If
$$v = \begin{bmatrix} v_1 \\ v_2 \end{bmatrix} \quad u = \begin{bmatrix} u_1 \\ u_2 \end{bmatrix}$$

Find v + u

4.   Define a Zero vector

5.   If $v = \begin{bmatrix} v_1 \\ v_2 \end{bmatrix}$, find α v

8   Numerical analysis

Numerical analysis is the branch of mathematics dealing with development and analysis of computational methods in approximation theory.

Numerical analysis is used for developing techniques to find a solution of mathematical equations, which describes a mathematical model. Such model is a formulation of the problem describing a physical situation. A numerical method which is used to solve a problem is often called an Algorithm. An algorithm is a set of procedures leading to a solution of a mathematical problem. Such a solution will be affected by errors, which need to be estimated. The final phase in solving a problem is programming, where the algorithm is transformed into a set of instructions for the computer. In this chapter we will look at various numerical methods and assess them in terms of accuracy.

8.1   Polynomial interpolation

Polynomials are widely used in numerical analysis because they have good approximating properties, easy to evaluate and easy to manipulate.

If we have n pairs of numbers (x_i, y_i) derived from the function $y=f(x)$ and we want to find the value of $f(x)$ for the intermediate values of x from the n pairs, then this process is known as interpolation. If we assume that the x_i are arranged in increasing order, then the nth degree polynomial $P_n(x)$, given $y_i=P_n(x_i)$ for n+1 successive values of i, is known as interpolating polynomial. On the other hand if we want to find the value of y beyond x_n, then the process is known as extrapolation.

8.1.1   Linear interpolation

The simplest interpolation is known as linear interpolation, which is a straight line joining two points (x_0, y_0) and (x_1, y_1) and the value of y for any x where x is $x_0 < x < x_1$.
See Fig 8.1.1-1 below.

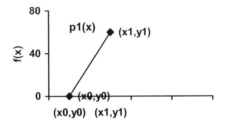

Fig. 8.1.1-1

A first degree polynomial can be written as follows:

$$p_1(x) = \left(\frac{x - x_1}{x_0 - x_1}\right) f(x_0) + \left(\frac{x - x_0}{x_1 - x_0}\right) f(x_1) \qquad (8.1.1.1)$$

Where the values of f(x) are given at x_0 and x_1. Equation (8.1.1.1) can be written as follows:

$$p_1(x) = \frac{(x - x_0) f(x_1) - (x - x_1) f(x_0)}{x_1 - x_0} \qquad (8.1.1.2)$$

8.1.2   Lagrange Interpolation

If we consider a general form of (8.1), we can write p_n in the form

$$p_n(x) = L_0(x)f(x_0) + L_1(x)f(x_1) + ... + L_n(x)f(x_n) \qquad (8.1.2.1)$$

Where $L_i(x) \in P_n$. The polynomial p_n will have the same values as the function f at $x = x_0, x_1, ..., x_n$ if $L_i(x) = \partial_{ij}$, $0 \le i \le n \partial_{ij}$ is the Kronecker delta function which is $=0$ when $i \ne j$ and 1 when $i = j$, therefore we have

$$l_0(x) = \frac{(x - x_1)}{(x_0 - x_1)} \frac{(x - x_2)...(x - x_n)}{(x_0 - x_2)....(x_0 - x_n)},$$

i.e. $l_0(x) = \displaystyle\prod_{j-1}^{n} \left(\frac{x - x_j}{x_0 - x_j} \right)$, and in general we have

$$l_i(x) = \prod_{\substack{j=0 \\ j \ne i}}^{n} \left(\frac{x - x_j}{x_i - x_j} \right) \qquad (8.1.2.2)$$

The interpolating polynomial can then be written in the following form, which is known as Lagrange interpolating polynomial.

$$P_n(x) = \sum_{i=0}^{n} L_i(x)f(x_i) \qquad (8.1.2.3)$$

Where $\qquad L_i(x) = \displaystyle\prod_{\substack{j=0 \\ j \ne i}}^{n} \frac{x - x_j}{x_i - x_j}, i = 0,...,n$

Expanding we have,

$$P(x) = \frac{(x - x_2)(x - x_3)...(x - x_n)}{(x_1 - x_2)(x_1 - x_3)...(x_1 - x_n)} y_1$$

$$+\frac{(x-x_1)(x-x_3)...(x-x_n)}{(x_2-x_1)(x_2-x_3)...(x_2-x_n)}y_2+...$$

$$+\frac{(x-x_1)(x-x_2)...(x-x_{n-1})}{(x_n-x_1)(x_n-x_2)...(x_n-x_{n-1})}y_n \qquad (8.1.2.4)$$

For $n = 3$ points,

$$P(x)=\frac{(x-x_2)(x-x_3)}{(x_1-x_2)(x_1-x_3)}y_1+\frac{(x-x_1)(x-x_3)}{(x_2-x_1)(x_2-x_3)}y_2+\frac{(x-x_1)(x-x_2)}{(x_3-x_1)(x_3-x_2)}y_3 \quad (8.1.2.5)$$

Note that the function $P(x)$ passes through the points, (x_i, y_i) as can be seen for the case $n = 3$,

$$P(x_1)=\frac{(x_1-x_2)(x_1-x_3)}{(x_1-x_2)(x_1-x_3)}y_1+\frac{(x_1-x_1)(x_1-x_3)}{(x_2-x_1)(x_2-x_3)}y_2+\frac{(x_1-x_1)(x_1-x_2)}{(x_3-x_1)(x_3-x_2)}y_3=y_1 \quad (8.1.2.6)$$

$$P(x_2)=\frac{(x_2-x_2)(x_2-x_3)}{(x_1-x_2)(x_1-x_3)}y_1+\frac{(x_2-x_1)(x_2-x_3)}{(x_2-x_1)(x_2-x_3)}y_2+\frac{(x_2-x_1)(x_2-x_2)}{(x_3-x_1)(x_3-x_2)}y_3=y_2 \quad (8.1.2.7)$$

$$P(x_3)=\frac{(x_3-x_2)(x_3-x_3)}{(x_1-x_2)(x_1-x_3)}y_1+\frac{(x_3-x_1)(x_3-x_3)}{(x_2-x_1)(x_2-x_3)}y_2+\frac{(x_3-x_1)(x_3-x_2)}{(x_3-x_1)(x_3-x_2)}y_3=y_3 \quad (8.1.2.8)$$

8.1.3   Horner`s Method

Horner's method (or synthetic division) is a technique for evaluating polynomials. Let P(x) be a polynomial of degree n given by the following form:

$$P_n(x) = a_{n+1}x^n + a_n x^{n-1} + ... + a_2 x + a_1 \qquad (8.1.3.1)$$

Consider evaluating $P_n(r)$, where r is a value of x. Dividing $P_n(x)$ by (x-r) we get a quotient polynomial $q_{n-1}(x)$ of degree n-1, and a remainder z.

$P_n(x)/(x-r) = q_{n-1}(x)$

$P_n(x) = (x-r) q_{n-1}(x) + z \qquad (8.1.3.2)$

$$q_{n-1}(x) = b_n x^{n-1} + b_{n-1}x^{n-2} + ... + b_3 x^2 + b_2 x + b_1 \qquad (8.1.3.3)$$

Substituting in (8.1.3.2) using (8.1.3.3), we get

$$P_n(x) = (x-r)(b_n x^{n-1} + b_{n-1}x^{n-2} + ... + b_3 x^2 + b_2 x + b_1) + z, (8.1.3.4)$$

$$=$$

$$b_n x^n + (b_{n-1} - rb_n)x^{n-1} + ... + (b_2 - rb_3)x^2 + (b_1 - rb_2)x + (z - rb_1)$$

Equating the coefficients of (8.1.3.1) and (8.1.3.4), we have:

$b_n = a_{n+1}$

$b_{n-1} - rb_n = a_n$

.....

$b_2 - rb_3 = a_3$

$b_1 - rb_2 = a_2$

$z - rb_1 = a_1$ and the coefficients of the quotient polynomial $q_{n-1}(x)$ are:

$b_n = a_{n+1}$

$b_{n-1} = a_n + rb_n$

.....

$b_2 = a_3 + rb_3$

$b_1 = a_2 + r b_2$

$z = a_1 + r b_1$

The evaluation of P(x) at x = r (by hand computations) would be as follows:

a_{n+1} a_n $a_{n-1} ...$ a_2 a_1 Coefficients of P(x)

rb_n	rb_{n-1}	$\ldots rb_2$	rb_1		
b_n	b_{n-1}	$b_{n-2}\ldots$	b_1	z	Coefficients of $q_{n-1}(x)$

Example 1: Given $P_3(x) = x^3 - 2x^2 - 2x - 3$

Evaluate $P_3(1)$
Following the method above we have:

1	-2	-2	-3
	1	-1	-3
1	-1	-3	$-6 = z$

Therefore $z = P_3(1) - -6$ and
$q_2(x) = x^2 - x - 3$

Example 2:

Find P (3) for the polynomial
$P(x) = x^5 - 6x^4 + 8x^3 + 8x^2 + 4x - 40$
Solution:

a_5	a_4	a_3	a_2	a_1	a_0
1	-6	8	8	4	-40
	3	-9	-3	15	57
1	-3	-1	5	19	$17 = P(3) = b_0$

The above example has been solved using Mathematica as shown below:

First, find Horner's nested form of the polynomial.

```
Clear[A, B, H, k, n, P, Q, x];
P[x_]=x^5-6x^4+8x^3+8x^2+4x-40;
Q[x_]=-40+(4+(8+(8+(-6+x)x)x)x)x;
A=coefficientlist[p[x],x];
n=length [A];
```

```
H[x_]:= Module[{},
B=Table[0,{n}];
B[[n]]=A[[n]];
For[k=n-1,1<=k,k- -,
B[[n]]=A[[k]]+xB[[k+1]]];
Return[B[[1]]];
Print [``P[3] = ``,P[3] ]
```

P[3] = 17

8.1.3.1 The Method of Least Squares

The method of **least squares** is most commonly used to calculate the coefficients of the interpolating polynomial. The method of least squares assumes that the best-fit curve of a given type is the curve that has the minimal sum of the deviations squared (Least Square error) from a given set of data. Suppose that the data points are (x_1, y_1), (x_2, y_2),..., (x_n, y_n), where x is the independent variable and y is the dependent variable. The fitting curve $f(x)$ has the deviation (error) d from each data point, i.e., $d_n = y_n - f(x_n)$. According to the method of least squares (see Annex 2), the best fitting curve has the property that:

$$\Pi = d_1^2 + d_2^2 + ... + d_n^2 = \sum_{i=1}^{n} d_i^2 = \sum_{i=1}^{n} \left[y_i - f(x_i) \right]^2 = \min$$

8.1.3.2   Polynomials Least-Squares Fitting

Polynomials are one of the most commonly used types of curves in regression.

The Least-Squares Line: The least-squares line method uses a straight line $y=a+bx$ to approximate the given set of data, (x_1,y_1), (x_2,y_2), ..., (x_n,y_n), , where n ≥ 2. (See Annex 2 for complete derivation).

The Least-Squares Parabola: The least-squares parabola method uses a second degree curve $y=a+bx+cx^2$ to approximate the given set of data, (x_1,y_1), (x_2,y_2), ..., (x_n,y_n), where n ≥ 3. (See Annex 2 for complete derivation).

The Least-Squares m^{th} Degree Polynomials: The least-squares m^{th} degree Polynomials method uses mth degree polynomials $y=a_0+ a_1x+ a_2 x^2 + \ldots a_m x^m$ to approximate the given set of data, (x_1,y_1), (x_2,y_2), ..., (x_n,y_n), where n $\geq m+1$. (See Annex 2 for complete derivation).

Multiple Regression Least-Squares: Multiple regression estimates the outcomes which may be affected by more than one control parameter or there may be more than one control parameter being changed at the same time, e.g., $z=a+bx+cy$. (See Annex 2 for complete derivation).

Examples:

1. If $f(x)$ is given at points $x=x_0$, x_1 and x_2 write the interpolating polynomial p_2.

   Solution:

$$P_2(x) = \frac{(x-x_1)(x-x_2)}{(x_0-x_1)(x_0-x_2)}y_0 + \frac{(x-x_0)(x-x_2)}{(x_1-x_0)(x_1-x_2)}y_1 + \frac{(x-x_0)(x-x_1)}{(x_2-x_0)(x_2-x_1)}y_2$$

2. If $f(x)$ is given as = 0, -3 and 4 for x=1, -1 and 2 find the interpolating polynomial for the function.

Solution:

$$P_2(x) = \frac{(x-1)(x-2)}{(1+1)(1-2)}0 + \frac{(x-1)(x-2)}{(-1-1)(-1-2)}(-3) + \frac{(x-1)(x+1)}{(2-1)(2+1)}4$$
$$= (1/6)\,(5x^2+9x-14)$$

3. Use linear interpolation on the values of log 2.1= 0.7419 and log2.2=0.7885, to estimate log 2.14.

Solution:

Calculate $p_1(x)$ from (8.1.1.1) with x_0 =2.1, x_1 =2.2, $f(x_0)$ =0.7419, $f(x_1)$ = 0.7885 and x =2.14. The result is that $p_1(2.14)$=0.76054, compared to the value of log2.14 = 0.76081.

8.1.4　Accuracy of interpolation

Considering the linear interpolation, we have
If P(x) denotes the linear polynomial interpolating f(x) at x_0 and x_1.

Then f(x)-P(x) $= \dfrac{(x-x_0)(x-x_1)}{2} f''(c_x) =$ Error   (8.1.4.1)

f(x) is twice differentiable on an interval *(a,b)* containing the points x_0, x_1 and $a \le x \le b$ and c_x falls between Min and Max of x_0, x_1 and *x.*

(8.1.4.1) becomes, if the points x_1, x *are near* $x_0,$

f(x)-P(x) $\approx \dfrac{(x-x_0)(x-x_1)}{2} f''(x_0) =$ Error approx. (8.1.4.2)

Example:

Consider example 3, in section 8.1.3.
f(x) = log 2.14, x_0 = 2.1, x_1 = 2.2, *x* = 2.14, P_1 = 0.76054 .

$$f''(x) = -\frac{\log e}{x^2} = -\frac{1}{x^2 \log(10)}$$

f(x)-P(x) $\approx \dfrac{(x-x_0)(x-x_1)}{2} \left[-\dfrac{1}{x^2 \log(10)} \right]$

=0.0012 ×0.0948324 = 0.00011379888
Copare with *f(2.14)* − *p(2.14)*= 0.76081-0.76054=0.00027

Gerneral case:
In general the error is estimated as follows:

$$f(x) - P_n(x) = \frac{(x-x_0)(x-x_1)...(x-x_n)}{(n+1)!} f^{(n+1)} c_x$$

Where c_x, falls between Min and Max of the points in $\{x, x_{0,...}, x_n\}$.
Let $\phi(x) = (x - x_0)(x - x_1)...(x - x_n)$ be a polynomial of degree
n+1 with roots $\{x_0, ..., x_n\}$.
Then we have

$$f(x) - P_n(x) = \frac{\phi(x)}{(n+1)!} f^{(n+1)} c_x$$

For n=2, we have

$$f(x) - P_2(x) = \frac{(x - x_0)(x - x_1)(x - x_2)}{3!} f^{(3)} c_x \qquad (8.1.4.3)$$

If we consider the case of evenly spaced nodes, we have
$x_1 - x_0 = h$, $x_2 - x_1 = h$ and assume $x_0 \leq x \leq x_2$
Then $\phi_2(x) = (x - x_0)(x - x_1)(x - x_2)$ can be computed for an x
value. The value of c_x in (8.14.3) is unknown, therefore we
replace $\left| f^{(3)} c_x \right|$ with a Max of $\left| f^{(3)}(x) \right|$, therefore we have:

$$\left| f(x) - P_2(x) \right| \leq \frac{\left| \phi_2(x) \right|}{3!} \max_{x_0 \leq x \leq x_2} \left| f^{(3)}(x) \right| \qquad (8.1.4.4)$$

For a uniform bond for $x_0 \leq x \leq x_2$, we compute

$$\max_{x_0 \leq x \leq x_2} \left| \phi_2(x) \right| = \max_{x_0 \leq x \leq x_2} \left| (x - x_0)(x - x_1)(x - x_2) \right|,$$

as follows:

$$\max_{x_0 \leq x \leq x_2} \left| \phi_2(x) \right| = \frac{2h^3}{3\sqrt{3}}, \qquad at \quad x = x_1 \pm \frac{h}{\sqrt{3}} \qquad (8.1.4.5)$$

From (8.1.4.4) and (8.1.4.5) we have

$$\left| f(x) - P_2(x) \right| \leq \frac{h^3}{9\sqrt{3}} \max_{x_0 \leq x \leq x_2} \left| f^{(3)}(x) \right|, \text{ for } x_0 \leq x \leq x_2 \qquad (8.1.4.6)$$

Example:

If we consider $f(x) = \log_{10} x$, with $1 \leq x_0 \leq x \leq x_2 \leq 10$
Using (8.1.4.6) we get

$$\left| \log_{10} x - P_2(x) \right| \leq \frac{h^3}{9\sqrt{3}} \max_{x_0 \leq x \leq x_2} \frac{2 \log_{10} e}{x^3} = \frac{0.05572 h^3}{x_0^{\,3}} \quad,$$

and if we assume h=0.01, we get

$$\left| \log_{10} x - P_2(x) \right| \leq \frac{5.57 \times 10^{-8}}{x_0^{\,3}} \leq 5.57 \times 10^{-8}$$

8.2   Numerical integration

To evaluate the definite integral $\int_a^b f(x)dx$, assuming f is integrable
, we develop the following methods:

8.2.1   The Midpoint rule

The definite intgral $\int_a^b f(x)dx$ can be approximated by the area of

the rectangle through midpoint x = (½)(a+b), which is equal to (b-a)f((½)(a+b)), as can be readily seen from Fig. 8.2.1-1.

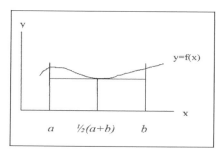

Fig. 8.2.1-1

Example:

Use the midpoint rule to approximate $\int_{1.5}^{2} \ell^x$

Solution: b – a = 2-1.5= 0.5

(b + a)/2 = 1.75

Approximation = 0.5f (1.75) = 2.8773

Compare with the exact value, which is = 2.907367

8.2.2   The Trapezium rule

The trapezium rule approximates an integral by the area of a trapezoid. The Trapezoidal Rule can be developed by approximating f(x) with a collection of line segments and integrate across each of these.

Let P be a partition of $[a,b]$ into n subintervals of equal width, $a=x_0 < x_1 <...< x_n =b$, where $x_i - x_{i-1} = (b-a)/n$ for i= 1,2 ...,n. On each subinterval we approximate $f(x)$ with a line segment. Here, we approximate $f(x)$ with the line segment that has the points x_{i-1}, $f(x_{i-1})$ and x_i, $f(x_i)$ and at its endpoints points that lie on the graph of $y = f(x)$. see Fig.8.2.2-1

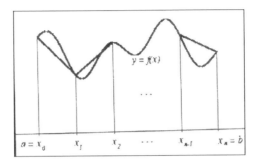

Fig. 8.2.2-1

Since exactly one line can pass through two distinct points, we see that any line that interpolates these points must be unique. Thus on (x_{i-1}, x_i) we approximate $f(x)$ with the unique line

$$y = \frac{f(x_i) - f(x_{i-1})}{x_i - x_{i-1}}(x_i - x_{i-1}) + f(x_{i-1})$$

Therefore

$$\int_{x_{i-1}}^{x_i} f(x)dx \approx \int_{x_{i-1}}^{x_i} \left(\frac{f(x_i)+f(x_{i-1})}{x_i-x_{i-1}}(x-x_{i-1})+f(x_{i-1}) \right)dx$$

By evaluating the integral on the right, we obtain

$$\int_{x_{i-1}}^{x_i} f(x)dx \approx \frac{\Delta x}{2}(f(x_i)+f(x_{i-1})),$$

since $\Delta x = (x_i - x_{i-1})$ for each i. Summing the definite integrals over each subinterval (x_{i-1}, x_i) we get the approximation

$$\int_{a}^{b} f(x)dx \approx \frac{\Delta x}{2}(f(x_1)+f(x_0))+\frac{\Delta x}{2}(f(x_2)+f(x_1))+...\frac{\Delta x}{2}(f(x_n)+f(x_{n-1}))$$

By simplifying this sum we obtain the approximation scheme

$$\int_{a}^{b} f(x)dx \approx \frac{\Delta x}{2}(f(x_0)+2f(x_1)+2f(x_2)+...+2f(x_{n-1})+f(x_n)) \quad (8.2.2.1)$$

(8.2.1) represents the Trapezoidal Rule. It is known by this name because on each subinterval (x_{i-1}, x_i) we are approximating the region bounded by the curve $y = f(x)$, the x-axis, and the lines x = x_{i-1} and x= x_i , with a region having a trapezoidal shape. Denote T_n to be the sum given on the right side of (8.2.2.1):

$$T_n = \frac{\Delta x}{2}(f(x_0)+2f(x_1)+2f(x_2)+...+2f(x_{n-1})+f(x_n))$$

Example 1

Approximate the value of the definite integral

$$\int_{-1}^{1} (1 - x^2)\,dx$$

by applying the Trapezoidal Rule with $n = 3$. Here we have $f(x) = 1 - x^2$, with $a = -1$ and $b = 1$, so that $\Delta x = 2/3$ with

$$x_i = -1 + \frac{2i}{3} = \frac{2i - 3}{3}$$

for $i = 0, 1, 2, 3$. When we apply the Trapezoidal Rule, we obtain

$$\int_{-1}^{1} (1 - x^2)\,dx \approx \frac{1}{2}(2/3)(f(-1) + 2f(-1/3) + 2f(1/3) + f(1))$$

$$= (1/3)(0 + 16/9 + 16/9 + 0 = 32/27$$

Note that the actual value of this integral is $4/3 = 1.333333333$.

Example 2

Apply the Trapezoidal Rule with $n = 6$ to approximate the value of

$$\int_1^2 \frac{1}{x}\,dx$$

In this case our function $f(x) = 1/x$, and we have $\Delta x = 1/6$ with

$$x_i = 1 + \frac{i}{6} = \frac{6-i}{6}$$

for $i = 0, 1, 2, 3, 4, 5, 6$. Applying the Trapezoidal Rule we have

$$\int_1^2 \frac{1}{x}\,dx \approx \frac{1}{12}(1 + 2(6/7) + 2(3/4) + 2(2/3) + 2(3/5) + 2(6/11) + 1/2)$$

$$= .694877345$$

Note that the actual value of this integral is $\ln(2) = 0.693147181$

Example 3

With $n = 9$ to approximate the value of

$$\int_1^e e^x \ln(x)\,dx$$

$f(x) = e^x \ln(x)$ and $\Delta x = (e-1)/9 = 0.191$ with

$$x_i = 1 + \frac{i(e-1)}{9}$$

for $i = 0, 1, 2, ...,9$. this yields the values of x_i and f(x) as shown in Table 8-1, from which we compute T9 .

Result : T_9 = 8.896083797

x_i	f(x)
1	0
1.190920203	0.574868251
1.381840406	1.287915841
1.572760609	2.182623220
1.763680813	3.310156060
1.954601016	4.732251791
2.145521219	6.524244600
2.336441422	8.778523818
2.527361625	11.608640254
2.718281828	15.154262241

Tabelle 8.2.2-1

In order to be more expedient and to produce successively better approximations by means of computing T_n for larger and larger values of n , having already computed T_n for some n, we wish to be able to find the next larger $N > n$ such that the amount of additional work required to compute T_n is minimized. To utilize the values of f(x) that we found in computing, this requires that N be a multiple of n, and thus we take $N = 2\,n$ to minimize the necessary additional work. We can compute T_{2n} from T_n according to the scheme

$$T_{2n} = \frac{1}{2}T_n + \frac{b-a}{2n}\sum_{i=1}^{2n-1} f(x_i) \quad \text{i is odd}$$

where $x_i = a + \dfrac{i(b-a)}{2n}$, $0 \leq i \leq 2n$

Therefore we need only find $f(x)$ at the additional n points. x_1, x_3, ..., x_{2n-1}.

instead of having to evaluate $f(x)$ at each of the $2n + 1$ points x_0, x_1, ..., x_{2n}.

8.2.2.1   Accuracy of the The Trapezoidal Rule

There is a possibility that the approximation will be exact, meaning that the amount of error, which is the difference between the exact value and the approximation, is 0. However, this is not true in general, and, in fact, for some functions this is impossible on particular intervals, an example of which will be given later on. We study the accuracy of an approximation by considering the error that it produces. Note that if we cannot find the exact value of a definite integral with a finite number of algebraic operations involving elementary functions, then neither can we find the exact value of the error of such an approximation scheme. However for some methods of approximation we can determine bounds for the magnitude of the error. While this does not explicitly give us the value of the error, it can still give us an estimate of how well we are able to approximate a given definite integral using such a method. For the Trapezoidal Rule we have the following

Theorem 1: *Suppose that $f''(x)$ exists on [a,b]. Then for n a positive integer,*

$$\int_a^b f(x)dx = T_n + E_n$$

where

$$T_n = \frac{b-a}{2n}(f(x_0)+2f(x_1)+2f(x_2)+...+2f(x_{n-1})+f(x_n))$$

and the error E_n is given by

$$E_n = -\frac{(b-a)^3}{12n^2}f''(c)$$

for some point c in [a,b].

Since the number c is not specified in this theorem, we are unable to use this to determine the exact value of E_n for functions $f(x)$ in general. However, one of the implications here is that the magnitude of the error has the bounds

$$\frac{(b-a)^3}{12n^2}\min_{a\leq x\leq b}|f''(x)|\leq |E_n|\leq \frac{(b-a)^3}{12n^2}\max_{a\leq x\leq b}|f''(x)|$$

Thus if $f''(x)$ is never 0 on [a,b], then the error E_n must be non-zero.

Example 4:

 In Example 2 we find T6 = 0.694877345 as an approximation of the value of

$$\int_1^2 \frac{1}{x}dx$$

For the function $f(x) = 1/x$, we have $f''(x) = 2/x^3$, so that

$$\frac{1}{432}\min_{1\le x\le 2}\frac{2}{x^3} \le |E_n| \le \frac{1}{432}\max_{1\le x\le 2}\frac{2}{x^3}$$

Since $f''(x)$ is strictly decreasing for all $x > 0$, we see that

$$.0005787 < \frac{1}{1728} \le |E_n| \le \frac{1}{216} < .0046297$$

Example 5:

In Example 3, we calculated T9 = 8.892367151 as an approximation of the value of

$$\int_1^e e^x \ln(x)\,dx$$

we get

$$f''(x) = e^x\left(\frac{2}{x} - \frac{1}{x^2} + \ln(x)\right)$$

Note that

$$f'''(x) = e^x\left(\frac{3}{x} - \frac{3}{x^2} + \frac{2}{x^3}\ln(x)\right)$$

which is positive for x ≥ 1. Therefore $f''(x)$ is increasing on $[1,e]$, so that

$$.0141876 < \frac{(e-1)^3}{972} f''(1) \leq |E_n| \leq \frac{(e-1)^3}{972} f''(e) < .1265863$$

8.2.3   Simpson`s rule

In this method we approximate $f(x)$ with a collection of arcs from quadratic functions and integrate across each of these. Let P be a partition of $[a,b]$ into n subintervals of equal width, P: $a=x_0 < x_1 <...< x_n =b$, where x_i-x_{i-1} = (b-a)/n for i= 1,2 ...,n.Here we require that n be even. Over each interval $\{x_{i-2}$, $x_i\}$, for i= 2,4...,n., we approximate $f(x)$ with a quadratic curve that interpolates the points$\{x_{i-2}$,$f(x_{i-2}\}$ $\{x_{i-1}$,$f(x_{i-1}\}\}$, and $\{x_i$,$f(x_i\}\}$.

Since only one quadratic function can interpolate any three (non-colinear) points, we see that the approximating function must be unique for each interval $\{x_{i-2}$, $x_i\}$. Note that the following quadratic function interpolates the three points
$\{x_{i-2}$,$f(x_{i-2}\}$ $\{x_{i-1}$,$f(x_{i-1}\}\}$, and $\{x_i$,$f(x_i\}\}$.

$$y = \frac{(x-x_{i-2})(x-x_{i-1})}{(x_i-x_{i-2})(x_i-x_{i-1})} f(x_i) +$$

$$\frac{(x-x_{i-1})(x-x_i)}{(x_{i-2}-x_{i-1})(x_{i-2}-x_i)} f(x_{i-2}) +$$

$$\frac{(x-x_i)(x-x_{i-2})}{(x_{i-1}-x_i)(x_{i-1}-x_{i-2})} f(x_{i-1})$$

Since this function is unique, this must be the quadratic function with which we approximate $f(x)$ on $\{x_{i-2}, x_i\}$. Also, if the three interpolating points all lie on the same line, then this function reduces to a linear function. Therefore, since $\Delta x = x_i - x_{i-1}$ for each i,

$$\int_{x_{i-2}}^{x_i} f(x)dx \approx \frac{1}{2(\Delta x)^2} \int_{x_{i-2}}^{x_i} \{\ (x-x_{i-2})(x-x_{i-1})f(x_i)$$

$$+\ (x-x_{i-1})(x-x_i)f(x_{i-2})$$

$$-\ 2(x-x_i)(x-x_{i-2})f(x_{i-1})\ \}dx$$

By evaluating the integral on the right, we obtain

$$\int_{x_{i-2}}^{x_i} f(x)dx \approx \frac{\Delta x}{3}(f(x_i)+4f(x_{i-1})+f(x_{i-2})$$

Summing the definite integrals over each interval (x_{i-2}, x_i), for $i=2,4,\ldots,n$, provides the approximation

$$\int_{a}^{b} f(x)dx \approx \frac{\Delta x}{3}(f(x_2)+4f(x_1)+f(x_0)$$

$$+\ \frac{\Delta x}{3}(f(x_4)+4f(x_3)+f(x_2))$$

$$+ \ldots + \frac{\Delta x}{3}(f(x_n) + 4f(x_{n-1}) + f(x_{n-2}))$$

By simplifying this sum we obtain the following approximation.

$$\int_a^b f(x)dx \approx \frac{\Delta x}{3}(f(x_0) + 4f(x_1) + 2f(x_2)$$

$$+ 4f(x_3) + \ldots 4f(x_{n-1}) + f(x_n)), \qquad (8.2.3.1)$$

which is the Simpson's Rule.

Example 1:

Apply Simpson's Rule with $n = 6$ to approximate the value of

$$\int_1^2 \frac{1}{x}dx$$

We have $\Delta x = 1/6$ and

$x_i = 1 + i/6$ for i= 0,1,2,…., 6.

Simpson's Rule (8.2.3.1) gives

$$\int_1^2 \frac{1}{x} dx \approx$$

1/18(1+4(6/7)+2(3/4)+4(2/3)+2(3/5)+4(6/11)+1/2)=0.693147181

Example 2:

Apply Simpson's Rule with $n = 8$ to approximate the value of

$$\int_1^e e^x \ln(x) dx$$

$\Delta x = (e - 1)/8 = 0.215$ and $x_i = 1 + i(e - 1)/8$ for i = 0,1, 2, … 8,

and we have the following values for x_i and $f(x)$.

x_i	$f(x)$
1	0
1.214785229	0.655608177
1.429570457	1.492717203
1.644355686	2.575108450
1.859140914	3.980031703
2.073926143	5.803451205
2.288711371	8.165809697
2.503496600	11.218892803
2.718281828	15.154262241

Applying Simpson's Rule using the above values we get

$$\int_{1}^{e} e^x \ln(x)dx \approx 8.837955521$$

Using the Excel Macro below (which may be adapted for similar problems) we get the following data in Table 8.2.3-1.

n	h	x	f(x)	Simpson
0	0.214785229	1.000000000	0.000000000	**8.837955521**
1	0.214785229	1.214785229	0.655608177	
2	0.214785229	1.429570457	1.492717203	
3	0.214785229	1.644355686	2.575108450	
4	0.214785229	1.859140914	3.980031703	
5	0.214785229	2.073926143	5.803451205	
6	0.214785229	2.288711371	8.165809697	
7	0.214785229	2.503496600	11.218892803	
8	0.214785229	2.718281828	15.154262241	

Tabelle 8.2.3-1

```
Sub Makrosimpson()
'
' Makrosimpson Makro
' Makro am 06/07/2005 von Yousif aufgezeichnet
'
'
  Range("A1").Select
  ActiveCell.FormulaR1C1 = "n"
  Range("B1").Select
  ActiveCell.FormulaR1C1 = "h"
  Range("C1").Select
  ActiveCell.FormulaR1C1 = "x"
  Range("D1").Select
  ActiveCell.FormulaR1C1 = "f(x)"
  Range("E1").Select
  ActiveCell.FormulaR1C1 = "S"
  Range("A2").Select
  ActiveCell.FormulaR1C1 = "0"
  Range("A3").Select
  ActiveCell.FormulaR1C1 = "1"
  Range("A4").Select
```

```
        ActiveCell.FormulaR1C1 = "2"
        Range("A5").Select
        ActiveCell.FormulaR1C1 = "3"
        Range("A6").Select
        ActiveCell.FormulaR1C1 = "4"
        Range("A7").Select
        ActiveCell.FormulaR1C1 = "5"
        Range("A8").Select
        ActiveCell.FormulaR1C1 = "6"
        Range("A9").Select
        ActiveCell.FormulaR1C1 = "7"
        Range("A10").Select
        ActiveCell.FormulaR1C1 = "8"
        Range("B2").Select
        ActiveCell.FormulaR1C1 = "=((EXP(1))-1)/8"
        Selection.Copy
        Range("B3:B10").Select
        ActiveSheet.Paste
        ActiveSheet.Paste
        Application.CutCopyMode = False
        Range("C2").Select
        ActiveCell.FormulaR1C1 = "=1+(RC[-2]*EXP(1)-(1*RC[-2]))/8"
        Range("C2").Select
        Selection.Copy
        Range("C3:C10").Select
        ActiveSheet.Paste
        ActiveSheet.Paste
        Application.CutCopyMode = False
        Range("B2").Select
        ActiveCell.FormulaR1C1 = "=1+(RC[-2]*EXP(1)-(1*RC[-2]))/8"
        Range("C2").Select
        Selection.Copy
        Range("C3:C10").Select
        ActiveSheet.Paste
        ActiveSheet.Paste
        Application.CutCopyMode = False
        Range("D2").Select
        ActiveCell.FormulaR1C1 = "=(LN(RC[-1]))*EXP(RC[-1])"
        Range("D2").Select
        Selection.Copy
        Range("D3:D10").Select
        ActiveSheet.Paste
        ActiveSheet.Paste
        Application.CutCopyMode = False
        Range("E2").Select
        ActiveCell.FormulaR1C1 = _
          "=(RC[-3]/3)*(RC[-1]+4*R[1]C[-1]+2*R[2]C[-1]+4*R[3]C[-1]+2*R[4]C[-1]+4*R[5]C[-
1]+2*R[6]C[-1]+4*R[7]C[-1]+R[8]C[-1])"
        Range("E2").Select
        Selection.Font.Bold = True
    End Sub
```

```
Sub Makro3()
'
' Makro3 Makro
' Makro am 06/07/2005 von Yousif aufgezeichnet
'
'
    Range("B3").Select
    Selection.Copy
    Range("B2").Select
    ActiveSheet.Paste
    ActiveSheet.Paste
    Application.CutCopyMode = False
End Sub
```

Example 3:

Find the approximate value of the definite integral

$$\int_0^1 \frac{1}{x^2+1} dx = \pi/4$$

Applying Simpson's Rule with $n = 2, 4, 6, 8,$ and 10.

n	S_n	Error
2	.783333333	.002064830
4	.785392157	.000006007
6	.785397945	.000000218
8	.785398126	.000000038
10	.785398153	.000000010

Tabelle 8.2.3-2

S_n (Simpson's Rule)values are converging to the value $\pi/4$ at a must faster rate than the values T_n (Trapezoidal rule).

8.2.3.1   Accuracy of Simpson's Rule

We now wish to examine how accurately Simpson's Rule approximates the definite integral of $f(x)$ on $[a,b]$. In this case the following has been proven:

Theorem 1 *Suppose that $f^{(4)}(x)$ exists on $[a,b]$. Then for n an even positive integer,*

$$\int_a^b f(x)dx = S_n + E_n,$$

where $S_n \approx \dfrac{b-a}{3n}(f(x_0) + 4f(x_1) + 2f(x_2)$

$$+ 4f(x_3) + ... + 4f(x_{n-1}) + f(x_n),$$

and the error E_n is given by

$$E_n = \frac{(b-a)^5}{180n^4} f^{(4)}(c)$$

for some point c in $[a,b]$.

the number c is not specified, and so we are not able to use this result to determine the exact value of E_n for most functions $f(x)$. However, we can see that the magnitude of the error has the bounds

$$\frac{(b-a)^5}{180n^4} \min_{a \le x \le b} |f^{(4)}(x)| \le E_n | \le \frac{(b-a)^5}{180n^4} \max_{a \le x \le b} |f^{(4)}(x)|$$

Example 4:

Find bounds on the error using Simpson's Rule with $n = 6$ to approximate the value of

$$\int_1^2 \frac{1}{x} dx$$

$f^{(4)}(x) = 24/x^5$, and we have

$$\frac{1}{233280} \min_{1 \le x \le 2} \frac{24}{x^5} \le E_n | \le \frac{1}{233280} \max_{1 \le x \le 2} \frac{24}{x^5}$$

Now, $f^{(4)}(x)$ is strictly decreasing for all $x > 0$, so that

$$.0000003215 < \frac{1}{311040} \le E_n | \le \frac{1}{9720} < .000102881$$

Example 5:

Find bounds on the error using Simpson's Rule with $n = 8$ to approximate the value of

$$\int_1^e e^x \, In(x) \, dx$$

with $n = 8$, we have

$$f^{(4)}(x) = e^x \left(\frac{4}{x} - \frac{6}{x^2} + \frac{8}{x^3} - \frac{6}{x^4} \right) + In(x)$$

It can be shown that $f^{(5)}(x) \geq 0$ for $x \geq 1$. Therefore $f^{(4)}(x)$

is increasing on $[1,e]$, and so

$$0 = \frac{(e-1)^5}{737280} f^{(4)}(1) \leq |E_n| \leq \frac{(e-1)^5}{737280} f^{(4)}(e) < .000600$$

The following *Mathematica* program applies Simpson's rule to approximate the area under a given curve $y = f(x)$ on an interval $[a,b]$. In its present form, it is written for the purpose of finding the area under the curve $y = e^x In(x)$ on the interval $[1,e]$ starting with $n = 6$ divisions of the interval. The program will continue to double the number of divisions until the magnitude of the difference between consecutive approximations of the definite integral is less than a given value (in this case .0005).

```
In(1)  f[x_]:=Exp[x]*Log[x]
a:=1.
b:=Exp[1.]
n:=6
If[Mod[n,2]==0,
Bn:=0;
Cn:=Sum[f[a+2*i*(b-a)/n],{i,1,(n-1)/2}];
sum1:=1.0;
sum2:=0.0;
While [Abs [sum2-sum1]>=.0005,
sum1=sum2;
```

```
delta=(b-a)/n;
Cn=Bn+Cn;
Bn=Sum[f[a+(2*i-1)*delta],{i,1,n/2}];
sum2=delta*(f[a]+f[b]+4*Bn+2*Cn)/3;
Print[n," ",N[sum2,20]];
n=2*n],
Print["The value of n, n = ",n,", is not even, and we cannot
proceed."]]
```

Out (1) 6   8.83851
     12   8.83775
     24   8.8377

8.2.4   Gaussian numerical integration

For a function $f(x)$ that is continuous on $[a,b]$, we refer to how well $f(x)$ can be approximated on $[a,b]$ by a polynomial of degree $\leq N$ by how small we can make the quantity

$$\max_{a \leq x \leq b} | f(x) - p(x) |, \qquad (8.2.4.1)$$

where $p(x)$ is some polynomial of degree $\leq N$. Note that we are referring to an approximation of $f(x)$ over all of the interval $[a,b]$, and not just at a finite set of points. Different polynomials $p(x)$ and $q(x)$ may yield different values for the expression given in (8.2.4.1), and $p(x)$ is said to be a better approximation of $f(x)$ on $[a,b]$ than $q(x)$ if

$$\max_{a \leq x \leq b} | f(x) - p(x) | < \max_{a \leq x \leq b} | f(x) - q(x) |$$

For polynomials of degree $\leq N$, the one that best approximates $f(x)$ is the one for which (8.2.4.1) is minimized. As N increases we would expect that $f(x)$ can be better approximated by polynomials of degree $\leq N$.

Let us consider how we might find the exact value of the definite integral

$$\int_{-1}^{1} p(x)dx$$

where $p(x)$ is a polynomial of a given degree. Note that the interval over which we are integrating is $[-1,1]$. Write this integral as a sum of weighted values of our function $p(x)$ evaluated at a particular set of nodes,

$$\int_{-1}^{1} p(x)dx = \sum_{i=1}^{n} w_i p(x_i) \qquad (8.2.4.2)$$

No initial restrictions on the weights w_i are made, but we require that the nodes x_i lie in the interval $[-1,1]$. This can be done for any function as long as the definite integral exists. For a given positive integer n, we wish to find a particular set of weights and nodes such that (8.2.4.2) will hold for all polynomials of as large a degree as possible. The largest such degree, say N, is called the degree of precision of the integration scheme. Now suppose that $f(x)$ is a function that can then be approximated on $[-1,1]$ by a polynomial $p(x)$ of degree $\leq N$. Then $p(x) \approx f(x)$ for each value of x in $[-1,1]$. Since the nodes, x_i, are each in $[-1,1]$, we have $p(x_i) \approx f(x_i)$ for each i. This implies that

$$\int_{-1}^{1} f(x)dx \approx \int_{-1}^{1} p(x)dx = \sum_{i=1}^{n} w_i p(x_i) \approx \sum_{i=1}^{n} w_i f(x_i)$$

Therefore we have

$$\int_{-1}^{1} f(x)dx \approx \sum_{i=1}^{n} w_i f(x_i) \qquad\qquad (8.2.4.3)$$

(8.2.4.3) is known as Gaussian numerical integration. Note that we do not need to know what polynomial can be used to approximate $f(x)$, but just that such a polynomial exists. If we have the values of the weights and the nodes for a given n, then we are able to approximate the definite integral as well as we could if we were to replace $f(x)$ with any polynomial of degree not exceeding the corresponding degree of precision N. Since the polynomial of degree $\leq N$ that will best approximate $f(x)$ must be included in this set, we have the best possible approximation over all such polynomials. Once we find the proper weights and nodes for each n, these will apply to any function $f(x)$.

Let us consider how to find the values of the weights and the nodes for a given value of n. For convenience, we shall use G_n to denote the sum given on the right side of (8.2.4.3) given a function $f(x)$:

$$G_n = \sum_{i=1}^{n} w_i f(x_i)$$

Considering the case for $n = 1$:

If $n = 1$, then (8.2.3.2) becomes

$$\int_{-1}^{1} p(x)dx = w_1 p(x_1) \qquad (8.2.4.4)$$

We now determine w_i and x_i so that (8.2.4.4) holds for all polynomials $p(x)$ of as large a degree as possible.

Let $p(x) = \alpha_0$, where $\alpha_0 \in \Re$. Then substituting this into (8.2.3.4),

$$\int_{-1}^{1} \alpha_0 dx = w_1 \alpha_0$$

Integrating and simplifying, we have

$2\alpha_0 = w_1 \alpha_0$

Therefore either $\alpha_0 = 0$ or $w_1 = 2$. In either case we can take $w_1 = 2$.

Now let $p(x) = \alpha_1 x + \alpha_0$, where $\alpha_0, \alpha_1 \in \Re$. When we substitute this, along with $w_1 = 2$, into (8.2.4.4), we obtain

$$\int_{-1}^{1} (\alpha_0 x + \alpha_0)dx = 2(\alpha_1 x_1 + \alpha_0)$$

Integrating and simplifying, we get

$2\alpha_1 x_1 = 0$.

Therefore either $\alpha_1 = 0$ or $x_1 = 0$. In either case we can take $x_1 = 0$.

Thus we see that (8.2.4.4) holds for all polynomials $p(x)$ of degree 1 or less if it is of the form

$$\int_{-1}^{1} p(x)dx = 2p(0) \qquad (8.2.4.5)$$

Since all weights and nodes have been determined at this point, we have, for an arbitrary function $f(x)$,

$$G_1 = 2f(0).$$

Note that (8.2.4.5) does not hold, in general, for polynomials $p(x)$ of degree 2 or greater, as we can illustrate with the example $p(x)=x^2$.

In this case we have

$$\int_{-1}^{1} x^2 dx = 2/3,$$

whereas $2p(0)=0$.

Therefore since (8.2.4.5) holds for all polynomials $p(x)$ of degree 1 or less, but does not hold for all polynomials of degree 2, the degree of precision of (8.2.4.5) is 1.

Example 1:

Use the Gaussian numerical integration with $n = 1$ to approximate the value of the definite integral

$$\int_{-1}^{1} \frac{1}{x+3} \, dx = In(2)$$

The value of this approximation will be the value of G_1 for the function $f(x) = 1/(x+3)$. We have

$$G_1 = 2f(0) = 2/3 \, ,$$

with an an error of .026480514.

Example 2:

Approximate the value of

$$\int_{-1}^{1} \cos(x) dx = 2\sin(1)$$

by applying Gaussian numerical integration with $n = 1$.

By (8.2.4.3) we have

$$\int_{-1}^{1} \cos(x) dx \approx 2\cos(0) = 2.$$

The error of this approximation is -.317058030.

Considering the case for $n = 2$:

For $n = 2$, (8.2.4.2) becomes

$$\int_{-1}^{1} p(x)dx = w_1 p(x_1) + w_2 p(x_2) \qquad (8.2.4.6)$$

For this case we determine the values of four unknowns, w_1, w_2, x_1 and x_2, so that (8.2.4.6) will hold for all polynomials $p(x)$ of as large a degree as possible.

We proceed much as we did for the case of $n = 1$ to find conditions on the four unknowns that will allow us to determine their values. Requiring (8.2.4.6) to hold for all polynomials of degree 0, implies

$$w_1 + w_2 = 2. \qquad (8.2.4.7)$$

This result, combined with the requirement that (8.2.4.6) holds for all polynomials of degree 1, implies that

$$w_1 x_1 + w_2 x_2 = 0. \qquad (8.2.4.8)$$

If (8.2.4.6) holds for all polynomials of degree 2 or less, then

$$w_1 x_1^2 + w_2 x_2^2 = 2/3. \qquad (8.2.4.9)$$

Finally, (8.2.4.7), (8.2.4.8), and (8.2.4.9), combined with (8.2.4.6) being true for all polynomials of degree 3, yields

$$w_1 x_1^3 + w_2 x_2^3 = 0. \qquad (8.2.4.10)$$

Thus we have four equations, (8.2.4.7), (8.2.4.8), (8.2.4.9), and (8.2.4.10), involving four unknowns, w_1, w_2, x_1 and x_2. We can combine this system to obtain the values $w_1 = w_2 = 1$, for the weights, and $x_1 = -x_2 = -\dfrac{\sqrt{3}}{3}$,

for the nodes. Therefore, (8.2.4.6) holds for all polynomials of degree 3 or less if it is of the form

$$\int_{-1}^{1} p(x)dx = p\left(-\frac{\sqrt{3}}{3}\right) + p\left(\frac{\sqrt{3}}{3}\right) \qquad (8.2.4.11)$$

Now, for an arbitrary function $f(x)$, we have

$$G_2 = f\left(-\frac{\sqrt{3}}{3}\right) + f\left(\frac{\sqrt{3}}{3}\right).$$

In general, polynomials of degree 4 or greater do not satisfy (8.2.4.11). Thus (8.2.4.11) has degree of precision 3.

8.3   Numerical differentiation

Numerical differentiation is the process of finding the numerical value of a derivative of a given function at a given point. There are many applications where derivatives need to be computed numerically. The simplest approach simply uses the definition of the derivative

$$f'(x) \equiv \lim_{h \to 0} \frac{f(x+h) - f(x)}{h} \qquad (8.3.1)$$

Then for small values of h, $D_{(h)}f(x)$ is a numerical approximation of $f'(x)$.

$$f'(x) = \frac{f(x+h) - f(x)}{h} \qquad (8.3.2)$$

Example 1:

Find an approximation of the derivative of $f(x) = e^x$ at $x = 2$ by finding $D_{(h)}f(x)$ with $h = .1$.

We have

$$D_{(.1)}f(2) = \frac{e^{2+.1} - e^2}{.1} = 10e^2(e^{.1} - 1)$$

This is $D_{(.1)}f(2) = 7.771138136$, compared with the actual value of the derivative which is $= 7.389056099$. This gives an error of -.382082037.

Example 2:

Consider the function $f(x) = \sqrt{1 - x^2}$ at the point $x = .5$. The actual value of the derivative is $f'(x) = -\sqrt{3}/3 = -0.57735027$. Approximating for various values of h we have,

$$D_{(h)}f(.5) = \frac{\sqrt{1-(x+h)^2} - \sqrt{1-x^2}}{h}$$

h	D(h)f(.5)	Error
0.1	-0.66025404	0.082903769
0.01	-0.58510029	0.007750017
0.001	-0.57812058	0.000770314
0.0001	-0.57742725	7.69852E-05
-0.1	-0.50489735	-0.07245292
-0.01	-0.56970291	-0.00764736
-0.001	-0.57658098	-0.00076929
-0.0001	-0.57727329	-7.6975E-05

The following Macro in Excel will print the above table. The Macro may be adapted for other similar problems.

```
Sub Macro1diff()
'
' Macro1diff Makro
' Macro am 06/07/2005 von Yousif aufgezeichnet
'

'
    Workbooks.Add
    Range("A1").Select
    ActiveCell.FormulaR1C1 = "h"
    Range("B1").Select
    ActiveCell.FormulaR1C1 = "D(h)f(.5)"
    Range("C1").Select
    ActiveCell.FormulaR1C1 = "Actual value"
    Range("A2").Select
    ActiveCell.FormulaR1C1 = "0.1"
    Range("A3").Select
    ActiveCell.FormulaR1C1 = "0.01"
    Range("A4").Select
    ActiveCell.FormulaR1C1 = "0.001"
    Range("A5").Select
    ActiveCell.FormulaR1C1 = "0.0001"
    Range("A6").Select
    ActiveCell.FormulaR1C1 = "-0.1"
    Range("A7").Select
    ActiveCell.FormulaR1C1 = "-0.01"
    Range("A8").Select
```

```
    ActiveCell.FormulaR1C1 = "-0.001"
    Range("A9").Select
    ActiveCell.FormulaR1C1 = "-0.0001"
    Range("B2").Select
    ActiveCell.FormulaR1C1 = "("
    Range("B2").Select
    ActiveCell.FormulaR1C1 = "=(((1-(0.5+RC[-1])^2)^0.5)-(1-0.5^2))/RC[-1]"
    Range("B2").Select
    ActiveCell.FormulaR1C1 = "=(((1-((0.5+RC[-1])^2))^0.5)-(1-0.5^2))/RC[-1]"
    Range("B2").Select
    ActiveCell.FormulaR1C1 = "=(((1-((0.5+RC[-1])^2))^0.5)-(1-0.5^2)^0.5)/RC[-1]"
    Range("C2").Select
    ActiveCell.FormulaR1C1 = "=-((3)^0.5)/3"
    Range("D1").Select
    ActiveCell.FormulaR1C1 = "Error"
    Range("D2").Select
    ActiveCell.FormulaR1C1 = "=RC[-1]-RC[-2]"
    Range("C1").Select
    Range("B2:D2").Select
    Selection.Copy
    Range("B3:D9").Select
    ActiveSheet.Paste
    ActiveSheet.Paste
    Application.CutCopyMode = False
    Windows("Mappe1").Activate
    Windows("Mappe2").Activate
    Range("I25").Select
End Sub
```

8.3.1   Central difference quotient.

Another method of numerically approximating the derivative, is the so called central difference quotient given by

$$D_{(h)}f(x) = \frac{f(x+h) - f(x-h)}{2h} \qquad (8.3.1.1)$$

Using the same above example for this method we get,

h	D(h)f(.5)	Error
0.1	-0.582575695	0.005225426
0.01	-0.577401598	5.13291E-05
0.001	-0.577350782	5.13201E-07
0.0001	-0.577350274	5.13153E-09
-0.1	-0.582575695	0.005225426
-0.01	-0.577401598	5.13291E-05
-0.001	-0.577350782	5.13201E-07
-0.0001	-0.577350274	5.13153E-09

Tabelle 8.3.1-1

with less error than the previous method.

If function $f(x)$ has n+1 continuous derivatives on an open interval (a,b), then using Taylor's series we have

$$f(z) = f(y) + f'(y)(z-y) + \frac{f''(y)}{2!}(z-y)^2$$

$$+ \ldots + \frac{f^{(n)}(y)}{n!}(z-y)^n + \frac{f^{(n+1)}(\xi)}{(n+1)!}(z-y)^n \qquad (8.3.1.2)$$

ξ is a point between z and y. Assuming $f(x)$ with two continuous derivatives and replacing z with $x+h$, y with x and sustituting in (8.3.1.2) we have

$$f(x+h) = f(x) + f'(y)h + \frac{f''(\xi)}{2!}h^2$$

and $$D_{(h)}f(x) = f'(x) + \frac{f''(\xi)}{2}h$$

The error of the numerical approzimation is given by

$$f'(x) - D_{(h)}f(x) = -\frac{f''(\xi)}{2}h$$

8.4   Solution of Agebriac equations

Here we develop numerical methods for solving equations of the form

$$f(x)=0, \qquad\qquad (8.4.1)$$

as follows:

8.4.1   Bisection method

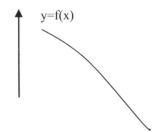

y=f(x)

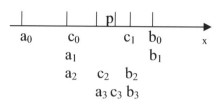

Fig. 8.4.1-1

Given a function f(x), we would like to find a value of x such that
$$f(x) = 0,$$

that is to say finding the root of the function f. the bisection method assumes that we have a starting interval, with a lower bound of x a_0 and an upper bound b_0,

The root is at $x=p$
The subintervals (a_n, b_n) for $n=1,2,\ldots$ contain the root p with $a_0, b_0 = (a, b)$

The Bisection Method provides a practical method to find roots of equation f(x) = 0,

Let $f(x)$ be a continuous function on the interval $[a, b]$. If $d \in [f(a), f(b)]$, then there is a $c \in [a, b]$ such that $f(c) = d$.
By replacing $f(x)$ by $f(x) - d$, we may assume that $d = 0$; it then suffices to obtain the following version:

Let $f(x)$ be a continuous function on the interval $[a, b]$. If $f(a)$ and $f(b)$ have opposite signs, then there is a $c \in [a, b]$ such that $f(c) = 0$. Here is an outline of its proof:

Let's assume that $f(a) < 0$, while $f(b) > 0$, the other case being handled similarly. Set $a_0 = a$ and $b_0 = b$.

Now consider the midpoint $m_0 = (a_0 + b_0)/2$, and evaluate $f(m_0)$. If $f(m_0) < 0$, set $a_1 = m_0$ and $b_1 = b_0$. If $f(m_0) > 0$, set $a_1 = a_0$ and $b_1 = m_0$. (If $f(m_0)=0$, then we have a root at m_0) $f(a_1)$ and $f(b_1)$ still have opposite signs, but the length of the interval $[a_1, b_1]$ is only half of the length of the original interval $[a_0, b_0]$. Note also that $a_0 \le a_1$ and that $b_0 \ge b_1$.

A further step: Consider the midpoint $m_1 = (a_1 + b_1)/2$, and evaluate $f(m_1)$. If $f(m_1) < 0$, set $a_2 = m_1$ and $b_2 = b_1$. If $f(m_1) > 0$, set $a_2 = a_1$ and $b_2 = m_1$. (If $f(m_1)=0$, then we have a root at m_0) $f(a_2)$ and $f(b_2)$ still have opposite signs, but the length of the interval $[a_2, b_2]$ is only a quarter of the length of the original interval $[a_0, b_0]$. Note also that $a_0 \le a_1 \ge a_2$ and that $b_0 \ge b_1 \ge b_2$.

Continuing in this fashion we construct by induction two sequences

$$(a_n)_{n=1}^{\infty} \le \text{ and } (b_n)_{n=1}^{\infty}$$

with the following properties:

1. (a_n) is an increasing sequence, (b_n) is a decreasing sequence.
2. $a_n \le b_n$ for all n.
3. $f(a_n) < 0$ for all n, $f(b_n) > 0$ for all n.
4. $b_n - a_n = 2^{-n}(b - a)$ for all n.

It follows from the first two properties that the sequences (a_n) and (b_n) converge; set

$$\lim_{n \to \infty} a_n = a, \quad \lim_{n \to \infty} b_n = b.$$

The third property and the continuity of the function $f(x)$ imply that $f(a) \leq 0$ and that $f(b) \geq 0$.

The crucial observation is the fact that the fourth property implies that $a = b$. Consequently, $f(a) = f(b) = 0$.

8.4.1.1   Bisection Theorem:

Intermediate Value Theorem:
If f is continuous on a closed interval $\{a, b\}$, and c is any number between $f(a)$ and $f(b)$ inclusive, then there is at least one number x in the closed interval such that $f(x) = c$.
The theorem is proven by observing that $f[\{a, b\}]$ is connected because the image of a connected set under a continuous function is connected, where $f[\{a, b\}]$ denotes the image of the interval $\{a, b\}$ under the function f. Since c is between $f(a)$ and $f(b)$, it must be in this connected set.

Assume that $f \in c(a, b)$ and that there exists a number $r \in (a,b)$ such that $f(r) = 0$.
If $f(a)$ and $f(b)$ have opposite signs, and (c_n) represents the sequence of midpoints generated by the bisection process, then

$$|r - c_n| \leq \frac{b-a}{2^{n+1}} \quad \text{for} \quad n=0,1,\ldots,$$

and the sequence c_n converges to the zero($x=r$).

That is, $\lim\limits_{k \to \infty} c_n = r$.

Example1.

Using the bisection method compute the square-root of 2.

Define
$f(x)=x^2-2$
Find x such that $f(x) =0$. That means the root of $f(x)$ will yield the square root of 2. The bisection method is an iterative algorithm that repeats until an acceptable error (ε) is acceptable. The steps for the algorithm are as follows:

i.   For the initial interval choose $x_L= 0$ and $x_U = 2$ for lower bound and upper bound respectively.
ii. Compute the middle point of the interval as
$$x_M = (x_L+ x_U)/2$$
iii. Compute the associated function at the end points as follows:
$$f_L= f(x_L) \text{ and } f_U= f(x_U)$$
iv. Compute the associated function at the end points as follows:
$$f_M= f(x_M)$$
v.   If $f_L < 0$ and $f_M < 0$ or if $f_L > 0$ and $f_M > 0$ then set $x_L= x_M$ and $f_L = f_M$.
vi. Other wise, set $x_U= x_M$ and $f_U = f_M$.

Applying the Algorithm, we have for n=10 iterations the following results:

n	x_L	f_L	x_U	f_U	x_M	f_M	ε
0	0	–	2	+	1	–	2
1	1	–	2	+	1.5	+	1
2	1	–	1.5	+	1.25	–	0.5
3	1.25	–	1.5	+	1.375	–	0.25
4	1.375	–	1.5	+	1.4375	+	0.125
5	1.375	–	1.4375	+	1.40625	–	0.0625
6	1.40625	–	1.4375	+	1.421875	+	0.03125
7	1.40625	–	1.421875	+	1.4140625	–	0.015625
8	1.4140625	–	1.421875	+	1.41796875	+	0.0078125
9	1.4140625	–	1.41796875	+	1.416015625	+	0.00390625
10	1.4140625	–	1.416015625	+	**1.415039063**	+	0.001953125

Tabelle 8.4.1-1

Approximate root =**1.415039063**
The root lies in {1.4140625, 1.416015625}.
The error of the approximation is:
½(x_U - x_L) =1/2(1.416015625-1.4140625) = 0.001953125

8.4.1.2   Advantages and disadvantages of the bisection method

The bisection method has the advantage that it always converges to a solution. However the method is slow to converge to a solution since a large number of iterations may be required to attain a small absolute error.

8.4.1.3   Mathematica Subroutine for the Bisection Method.

The following Mathematica code find the approximation of $\sqrt{2}$
where f(x) =x^2-2.

```
In[34]:=
Off[General::spell1];
Clear[Bisection, f0, a0, b0, delta, x];
Bisection[f0_, a0_, b0_, delta_, digits_] :=
Module[{a, b, c, Ya, Yb, Yc, f, k, cond, MaxIter, MethodDoesNotApply,
PerfectZero, RootInTolerance}, Set @@ {f[x_], f0};
a = N[a0, digits];
b = N[b0, digits];
k = 0;
Ya = f[a];
Yb = f[b];
dx = b - a;
cond = 0;
MaxIter = 11 // N;
If[Ya Yb > 0, cond = MethodDoesNotApply];
Print["\t", "\t    a = ", N[a, digits]];
Print["\t", "\t    b = ", N[b, digits]];
While[cond == 0 && k < MaxIter, c = (a + b)/2;
Yc = f[c];
Print["k = ", k, "\t    c = ", N[c, digits]];
If [Yc == 0, a = c; b = c; cond = PerfectZero];
If[Yb Yc > 0, b = c; Yb = Yc, a = c; Ya = Yc];
```

```
dx = b - a;
k = k + 1;];
If[dx < delta && cond != PerfectZero, cond = RootInTolerance];
Print[" "];
Print["The function is f[x] = ", f[x]];
Print["Estimated root c = ", N[c, digits]];];
On[General::spell1];
Clear[f, x];
f[x_] = x^2 - 2
Print["The function is f[x] = ", f[x]];
Plot[f[x], {x, 1, 2}, PlotLabel -> "The curve y = f(x)."];
Bisection[f[x], 0, 2, 10^-7, 11]
Out[39]=
```

$$f[x] = x^2 - 2$$

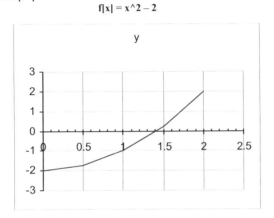

Fig. 8.4.1-2

$$b = 2.$$

K	C

0	1.
1	1.5
2	1.25
3	1.375
4	1.4375
5	1.40625
6	1.42188
7	1.41406
8	1.41797
9	1.41602
10	1.41504

Tabelle 8.4.1-2

The function is f[x] = -2 + x^2
Estimated root c = 1.41504

Example 2.

Find the roots of the polynomial $p(x) = x^7 + 9x^5 - 13x - 17$.

Note that $p(0)=-17$ and $p(2)=373$. Therefore, since $p(x)$ is a continuous function (i.e., its graph has no ``breaks"), we know that there must be a root, say r, in the interval $(0, 2)$.

To close in on r *(the root)*, we now evaluate p at the midpoint of $(0, 2)$ which is 1.and p (1)=-20. Now we see that r must actually lie in the interval $(1, 2)$ since p switches signs from negative to positive as x ranges from 1 to 2. So we have reduced the interval under consideration from $(0, 2)$ to $(1, 2)$. We have cut the length of our interval in half, or *bisected* it.
We look next at the midpoint of $(1, 2)$, namely 1.5 and p (1.5)= 48.929 . Thus, r must be in the interval $(1, 1.5)$. We continue this procedure until a desired accuracy has been achieved. Table 2 summarizes the results of iterations.

Left Endpoint	Right Endpoint	Midpoint	p(Midpoint)
0	2	1	-20
1	2	1.5	48.929
1	1.5	1.25	-1.015
1.25	1.5	1.375	18.651
1.25	1.375	1.3125	7.701
1.25	1.3125	1.28125	3.086
1.25	1.28125	1.265625	0.974
1.25	1.265625	1.2578125	-0.035
1.2578125	1.265625	1.26171875	0.465
1.2578125	1.26171875	1.259765625	0.213

Tabelle 8.4.1-3

Note that after these iterations are performed, we see that

$$1.2578125 < r < 1.259765625$$

Hence, we have been able to find r accurate to the hundredths place.

As mentioned before this method always converge to a root, provided that function under consideration is continuous and we begin with two values a and b such that $p(a)<0$ and $p(b)>0$. (The Intermediate Value Theorem (8.4.1.1) guarantees that a root exists under these conditions.)

Using the following Mathematica program for the above example we have:

```
In[35]:=
Off[General::spell1];
Clear[Bisection, f0, a0, b0, delta, x];
Bisection[f0_, a0_, b0_, delta_, digits_ ] :=
Module[{a, b, c, Ya, Yb, Yc, f, k, cond, MaxIter, MethodDoesNotApply,
PerfectZero, RootInTolerance}, Set @@ {f[x_], f0};
a = N[a0, digits];
b = N[b0, digits];
k = 0;
Ya = f[a];
Yb = f[b];
dx = b - a;
cond = 0;
MaxIter = 11 // N;
If[Ya Yb > 0, cond = MethodDoesNotApply];
```

```
Print["\t", "\t     a = ", N[a, digits]];
Print["\t", "\t     b = ", N[b, digits]];
While[cond == 0 && k < MaxIter, c = (a + b)/2;
Yc = f[c];
Print["k = ", k, "\t     c = ", N[c, digits]];
If [Yc == 0, a = c; b = c; cond = PerfectZero];
If[Yb Yc > 0, b = c; Yb = Yc, a = c; Ya = Yc];
dx = b - a;
k = k + 1;];
If[dx < delta && cond != PerfectZero, cond = RootInTolerance];
Print[" "];
Print["The function is f[x] = ", f[x]];
Print["Estimated root c = ", N[c, digits]];];
On[General::spell1];
Clear[f, x];
f[x_] = x^7+9 x^5 – 13x-17
Print["The function is f[x] = ", f[x]];
Plot[f[x], {x, 1, 2}, PlotLabel -> "The curve y = f(x)."];
Bisection[f[x], 1, 2, 10^-7, 11]
Out[35]=
```

f[x] = x^7+9 x^5 – 13x-17

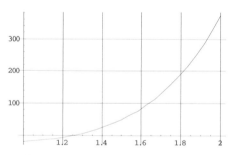

a = 1.

b = 2.

k	c

0	1.5
1	1.25
2	1.375
3	1.3125
4	1.28125
5	1.26563
6	1.25781
7	1.26172
8	1.25977
9	**1.25879**

The root c = 1.25879

8.4.2   Newton's Method

A second method of approximating roots of functions, we consider here is known as **Newton's method** (also know as Newton-Raphson Method). We need to assume that f is a differentiable function in some interval $[a, b]$, i.e., we can find f' in the interval $[a, b]$. We first consider Figure 8.4.2.-1 and see how Newton's method works.

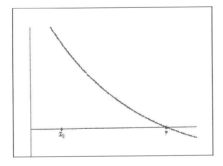

Fig. 8.4.2-1

We see a portion of the graph of f along with the root r and an additional point x_0 which will be referred to as a **seed value** (starting point). x_0 is our initial approximation of r. We now draw a vertical line segment from the seed value x_0 to the graph of f. See Fig.8.4.2-2.

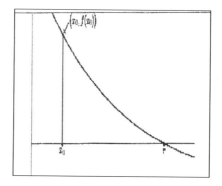

Fig. 8.4.2-2

We then draw the tangent line to the curve of f through $(x_0, f(x_0))$. This line crosses the x-axis at a new point, say x_1. See Fig.8.4.2-3.

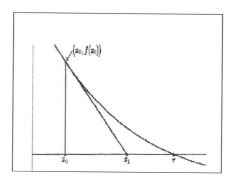

Fig. 8.4.2-3

Note that in Fig. 8.4.2-3, x_1 is a better approximation of r than x_0. We now iterate this process, yielding new points x_2, x_3, ... until we are "close enough" to r. Figure 3.4 shows one more iteration of this process, determining x_2.

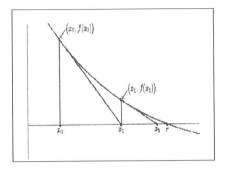

Fig. 8.4.2-4

Now we consider this method algebraically. Referring back to Fig. 8.4.2-3 we see that the slope of the line through the points $(x_1, 0)$ and $(x_0, f(x_0))$ is equal to

$$\frac{0 - f(x_0)}{x_1 - x_0}$$

Moreover, the slope also equals $f'(x_0)$ since this line is tangent to the curve of f. Hence,

$$f'(x_0) = \frac{-f(x_0)}{x_1 - x_0}$$

which yields

$$x_1 - x_0 = \frac{-f(x_0)}{f'(x_0)}$$

or $$x_1 = x_0 - \frac{f(x_0)}{f'(x_0)}$$

Iterating this yields the general term

$$x_{n+1} = x_n - \frac{f(x_n)}{f'(x_n)} \text{ for n=0,1,2,....} \quad (8.4.2.1)$$

This iterative technique is Newton's method and can be easily applied with the aid of a computer program.

The equation 8.4.2.1 can be also derived using Taylor's Theorem. Assume that function f and its derivatives up to f^{n+1} exist on an interval [a, b]. Let $x_0 \in$ [a, b]. Then for every x ∈ [a, b] there is a value $\phi(x)$ between x and x_0 such that

$$f(x) = f(x_0) + (x - x_0)f'(x_0) + \frac{(x - x_0)^2}{2!} f''(x_0) + ...$$

$$+ \frac{(x - x_0)n}{n!} f^{(n)}(x_0) + \frac{(x - x_0)n+1}{(n+1)!} f^{(n+1)}(\phi(x)) \quad (8.4.2.1)$$

The last term of equation (8.4.2.1) is the remainder term. The Newton's method is derived from (8.4.2.1) by taking n = 1 and neglecting the remainder term. Therefore we have

$$f(x) \approx f(x_0) + (x - x_0)f'(x_0)$$

Solving for f(x) = 0, we have

$$x \approx x_0 - \frac{f(x_0)}{f'(x_0)}$$

The next approximation for the root x_1 is then

$$x_1 \approx x_0 - \frac{f(x_0)}{f'(x_0)}$$

We then use Taylor's Theorem to get x_2 till we get the general

Newton's formula, $x_{k+1} \approx x_k - \dfrac{f(x_k)}{f'(x_k)}$ as before.

8.4.2.1   Newton's Method to find the roots of a polynomial

For a polynomial $P_n(x)$, the roots are computed using the following iteration formula

$$x_{j+1} = x_j - \frac{P_n(x_j)}{P'_n(x_j)} \quad j = 0,1,2,\ldots$$

See example in 8.4.2.2 below.

8.4.2.2   Newton's method Algorithm

Input: Initial starting point, x_0
       Tolerance, ε
       Maximum number of iteration, N
Output: Approximate solution, x_1
       Or print message of failure.

1st step: Set $x_1 = x_0 - \dfrac{f(x_0)}{f'(x_0)}$

2nd step: Set counter $= 1$

3rd step: While $\left| x_1 - x_0 \right| > \varepsilon$ do steps 4-7

4th step: Set $x_0 = x_1$

5th step: Set $x_1 = x_0 - \dfrac{f(x_0)}{f'(x_0)}$

6th step: counter $=$ counter $+ 1$

7th step: If counter $> N$ then Output (`Method failed after` N `iterations). Stop

8th step: Output (x_1),
Stop.

Note: The method will fail if $f'(x_k) = 0$

Example:

Consider $p(x) = x^7 + 9x^5 - 13x - 17$ as in the previous example dealing with the bisection method. We have seen from the bisection method that one root of p lies in the interval $(1, 2)$. Using $x_0 = 1$ as our seed value, we can generate the following table via Newton's method.

n	x_n	$p(x_n)$	$p'(x_n)$	x_{n+1}
0	1	-20	39	1.512820513
1	1.512820513	52.78287188	306.6130739	1.340672368
2	1.340672368	12.33751268	173.0270062	1.269368397
3	1.269368397	1.46911353	133.1159618	1.258332053
4	1.258332053	0.03053547	127.6107243	1.258092767
5	1.258092767	0.00001407	127.4932403	**1.258092657**

Note that after 6 iterations of Newton's method, the root r (x_{n+1}) can be approximated as

r = 1.258092657, accurate to 9 decimal places.
The following simple Excel Macro print the above table. The Macro may be adapted for other problem of finding the roots.

```
Sub Newtonmethod()
'
' Newtonmethod Macro
' Macro recorded 15/07/2005 by Yousif
'


'
    Range("A1").Select
    ActiveCell.FormulaR1C1 = "N"
    Range("B1").Select
```

```
ActiveCell.FormulaR1C1 = "Xn"
Range("C1").Select
ActiveCell.FormulaR1C1 = "Px"
Range("D1").Select
ActiveCell.FormulaR1C1 = "P`x"
Range("E1").Select
ActiveCell.FormulaR1C1 = "Xn+1"
Range("A2").Select
ActiveCell.FormulaR1C1 = "0"
Range("A3").Select
ActiveCell.FormulaR1C1 = "1"
Range("A4").Select
ActiveCell.FormulaR1C1 = "2"
Range("A5").Select
ActiveCell.FormulaR1C1 = "3"
Range("A6").Select
ActiveCell.FormulaR1C1 = "4"
Range("A7").Select
ActiveCell.FormulaR1C1 = "5"
Range("B2").Select
ActiveCell.FormulaR1C1 = "1"
Range("C2").Select
ActiveCell.FormulaR1C1 = "=RC[-1]^7+9*RC[-1]^5-13*RC[-1]-17"
Range("D2").Select
ActiveCell.FormulaR1C1 = "=7*RC[-2]^6+45*RC[-2]^4-13"
Range("E2").Select
ActiveCell.FormulaR1C1 = "=RC[-3]-RC[-2]/RC[-1]"
Range("C2:E2").Select
Selection.Copy
Range("C3:E7").Select
ActiveSheet.Paste
ActiveSheet.Paste
Application.CutCopyMode = False
Range("B3").Select
ActiveCell.FormulaR1C1 = "=R[-1]C[3]"
Range("B3").Select
Selection.Copy
Range("B4:B7").Select
ActiveSheet.Paste
ActiveSheet.Paste
Application.CutCopyMode = False
' Newtonmethod Macro
' Stop Criteria
Range("F2").Select
ActiveCell.FormulaR1C1 = "=RC[-1]-RC[-4]"
Range("F2").Select
Selection.Copy
Range("F3:F7").Select
ActiveSheet.Paste
ActiveSheet.Paste
Application.CutCopyMode = False
```

```
Columns("F:F").ColumnWidth = 12
ActiveWindow.SmallScroll ToRight:=1
Range("F2").Select
ActiveCell.FormulaR1C1 = "=ABS(RC[-1]-RC[-4])"
Range("F2").Select
Selection.Copy
Range("F3:F7").Select
ActiveSheet.Paste
ActiveSheet.Paste
Application.CutCopyMode = False
Range("G2").Select
ActiveCell.FormulaR1C1 = "=IF(ABS(RC[-1])>0.00000012,""continue"","""stop"")"
Selection.Copy
Range("G3:G7").Select
ActiveSheet.Paste
ActiveSheet.Paste
Application.CutCopyMode = False
End Sub
```

Output:

N	Xn	Px	P`x	Xn+1	|Xn+1- Xn|	criteria
0	1	-20	39	1.512820513	0.512820513	continue
1	1.512820513	52.78287	306.6131	1.340672368	0.172148145	continue
2	1.340672368	12.33751	173.027	1.269368397	0.071303971	continue
3	1.269368397	1.469113	133.116	1.258332053	0.011036344	continue
4	1.258332053	0.030535	127.6107	1.258092767	0.000239286	continue
5	1.258092767	1.41E-05	127.4932	**1.258092657**	0.000000110	stop

$$\varepsilon = |0.00000012|$$

Using the above Macro adjusted to find the square root of 2 we have:

N	Xn	Px	P`x	Xn+1	|Xn+1- Xn|	criteria
0	1	-1	2	1.500000000	0.50000000000	continue
1	1.500000000	0.25	3	1.416666667	0.08333333333	continue
2	1.416666667	0.006944	2.833333	1.414215686	0.00245098039	continue
3	1.414215686	6.01E-06	2.828431	1.414213562	0.00000212390	continue
4	1.414213562	4.51E-12	2.828427	**1.414213562**	0.00000000000	stop

$$\varepsilon = |0.00000212|$$

Converge to the root much more rapidly than the bisection method.

Example:

Find $\sqrt{10}$ using Newton's method.

Solution:

Newton's iteration is $x_{k+1} = 1/2(x_k + \dfrac{10}{x_k})$,

Starting with $x_0 = 3$, we have

k x_k
0   3
1   3.166666666666670
2   3.162280701754390
3   3.162277660169840
4   3.162277660168380

8.4.3   Comparisons

In comparing the results of the previous two sections, we see that Newton's method appears to converge to the root *r* much more rapidly than the bisection method. In general, this is indeed the case. Newton's method does not always converge to the root, while the bisection method always does (so long as the function *f* is continuous and one begins with values *a* and *b* such that *f*(*a*) and *f*(*b*) are of different sign). A "poor" choice for the seed value x_0 may cause Newton's method to "miss" the root. The following example will clear this point. (if a "poor" choice for the seed value x_0.)

Example:

Consider the function

$$f(x) = (\ln x) / x^2$$

Note that f has one root at $x=1$ since $\ln 1 = 0$. The following table gives the results of applying Newton's method to this function with seed value $x_0 = 2$:

n	x_n	$f(x_n)$	$f'(x_n)$	x_{n+1}
0	2	0.1732867952	-0.0482867952	5.588699452
1	5.588699452	0.05509287184	-0.01398695752	9.527574062
2	9.527574062	0.02483281062	-0.004056576382	15.64919197
3	15.64919197	0.1123091313	-0.00117440443	25.21226310
4	25.21226310	0.00507714751	-0.000340355109	40.12946981

Note that, the estimates for the root are getting larger and larger; they will, in fact, continue to do this. The root $r=1$ is being completed missed.

The Newton-Raphson Method can be unreliable, If the algorithm encounters a point x where $f'(x) = 0$, it crashes; if it encounters points where the derivative is very close to 0, it will become very unreliable.

The Bisection Method on the other hand will always work, once you have found starting points a and b where the function takes opposite signs.

8.4.4   Fixed Point Theorem

If g is a continuous function $g(x) \in \{a, b\}$ for all $x \in \{a, b\}$, then g has a fixed point in $\{a, b\}$. This can be proven by noting that

$g(a) \geq a \;\; g(b) \leq b$

$g(a)\text{-}a \geq 0 \;\; g(b)\text{-}b \leq 0$

Since g is continuous, the intermediate value theorem guarantees that there exists a $c \in \{a, b\}$ such that

$g(c)\text{-}c=0,$

so there must exist a c such that

$g(c)=c$

so there must exist a fixed point$\in \{a, b\}$.

8.4.4.1 Uniqueness of fixed point

If ϕ is continuous on the interval $[a,b]$ and if $\phi(x) \in [a,b]$ for all $x \in [a,b]$ and ϕ' exists on the interval $[a,b]$ with $|\phi'(x)| \leq k < 1$, where k is a constant, and for all $x \in [a,b]$, then the fixed point in the interval $[a,b]$ is unique. This can be proved as follows:

Assume there are two fixed points X and Z, then by the mean value theorem (8.4.1.1) we have,

$$\frac{\phi(X) - \phi(Z)}{X - Z} = \phi'(\xi)$$

Where ξ fall between X and Z.

Now $|X\text{-}Z| = |\phi(X) - \phi(Z)| = |\phi'(\xi)| \, |X - Z|$

$\qquad\qquad < |X\text{-}Z|$, $\qquad\qquad\qquad\qquad\qquad$ (1)

$|\phi'(\xi)| < 1$. (8.4.4.1) reflects a contradiction; therefore there is only a fixed point.

Considering Newton's method we have

$$\phi(x) = x - \frac{f(x)}{f'(x)}$$

$$\phi'(X) = 0, \quad f'(X) \neq 0$$

i.e. Newton's method converges when $f'(X) \neq 0$ and with a suitable starting point.

The following example illustrates the Fixed Point iteration.

Find $\sqrt{5}$. For this case the equation would be,

$$x^2 - 5 = 0$$

Select $\phi(x)$ so that $|\phi'(X)| < 1$ for $x = \sqrt{5}$

$x^2 - 5 = 0$

$x^2 - 4 = 1$

$(x-2)(x+2) = 1$

$x-2 = 1/(x+2)$

$x = 2 + 1/(x+2)$

$\phi(x) = 2 + 1/(x+2)$

$\phi'(x) = -1/(x+2)^2 = -1/(\sqrt{5}+2)^2 = 0.055728$

Therefore the Fixed Point $x_{k+1} = (2x_k+5) / (x_k+2)$ will converge to $\sqrt{5}$.

8.4.4.2   Newton's Method using Matlab

```
Function x1 = Newton (x0, epsilon, n)
%Newton-Raphson algorithm for solving f(x) =0
%    NEWTON(X0, EPSILON, N) is the approximation to root1
%    x0 is the starting value1
%    EPSILON the tolerance for the difference of successive iterates
%    N the maximum number of iteration allowed
x1=x0-f(x0)/df(x0);
counter = 1
while asb(x1-x0) >epsilon
        x0 = x1;
        x1 = x0-f(x0)/df(x0);
```

counter = counter + 1;
if counter > n
error (`Newton method failed to converge in maximum allowed
iterations`)
end
end

8.4.5 Solving for quadratic roots.
Using Matlab.
Example:
Solving for quadratic roots
Solve for x: $2x^2 + 10x + 12 = 0$
Expressing the quadratic polynomial in parametric form:
$ax^2 + bx + c = 0$ (1)
if a $\neq 0$, rewrite (1)
$x^2 + bx/a + c/a = 0$ (2)
Completing the square, (2) becomes

$$\left(x+\frac{b}{2a}\right)^2 -\left(\frac{b}{2a}\right)^2 +\frac{c}{a} = 0$$

Rearrange as follows

$$\left(x+\frac{b}{2a}\right)^2 =\left(\frac{b}{2a}\right)^2 (b^2 - 4ac)$$

Take the square root of each side we have

$$x_{1,2} = \frac{b}{2a} \pm \frac{1}{2a}\sqrt{b^2 - 4ac}$$

There are two solutions, and to develop the Matlab command we
rewrite the equation in the following format:
$Y = -b/2a$
$$Z = \frac{1}{2a}\sqrt{b^2 - 4ac}$$
$X_1 = y + z$
$X_2 = y - z$
Matlab session:

```
>> a=2;
>> b=10;
>> c=12;
>> y=-b/(2*a);
>> z=sqrt(b*2-4*a*c)/(2*a);
>> x1=y+z
x1=
          -2
>> x2=y-z
x2=
          -3
```
The roots are: -2 and -3.

8.4.6   Secant method

Secant method for f(x) = 0
The secant method may be derived from Newton's method by approximating the derivative of f(x) at two points x_n and x_{n-1} by

$$f'(x) = \frac{f(x_n) - f(x_{n-1})}{x_n - x_{n-1}}$$

Geometrically, Newton's method uses the tangent line and the secant method approximates the tangent line by a secant line.
Secant Method is a root-finding algorithm which assumes a function to be approximately linear in the region of interest. Each improvement is taken as the point where the approximating line crosses the axis. The secant method retains only the most recent estimate.

$$f'(x_{n-1}) \approx \frac{f(x_{n-1}) - f(x_{n-2})}{x_{n-1} - x_{n-2}} \tag{1}$$

$$f(x_n) \approx f(x_{n-1}) + f'(x_{n-1})(x_n - x_{n-1}) = 0 \tag{2}$$

$$f(x_{n-1}) + \frac{f(x_{n-1}) - f(x_{n-2})}{x_{n-1} - x_{n-2}}(x_n - x_{n-1}) = 0, \qquad (3)$$

$$x_n = x_{n-1} - \frac{f(x_{n-1})(x_{n-1} - x_{n-2})}{f(x_{n-1}) - f(x_{n-2})}, \qquad (4)$$

(4) gives the iteration scheme.

Mathematica uses *FindRoot* to estimate the derivative of your functions numerically. The approach it uses is based on the `secant method`. One feature of this method is that to get it started, you have to specify the first two values.

Example 1: Find the square root of 2

Mathematica output:

SecantMethod[f0_, x0_, x1_, delta_, epsilon_, max_, digits_]
f0_ the function f(x),
x0_ the starting value,
x2_, x1_ the starting values,
delta_ estimate for the accuracy of the solution,
epsilon_ estimate for the magnitude of f(x),
max_ the maximum number of iterations,
digits_ the number of digits displayed in the output

Initial values are 0 and 1
FindRoot[x^2-2=0,{x,{0,1}}]
{x = 1.41421}
The results of the iterations are:

n	x
0	0

1	1
2	2.0000000000000
3	1.3333333333333
4	1.4000000000000
5	1.4146341463415
6	1.4142114384749
7	1.4142135620573
8	**1.4142135623731**

Example 2:

Find root 5.

Initial values are 1.5 and 2.

f[x_] = $x^2 - 5$;

SecantMethod[f0_, x0_, x1_, delta_, epsilon_, max_, digits_]

{x = -2.23607}

The results of iterations are:

n	x
0	1.5
1	2
2	2.2857142857142856
3	2.2333333333333334
4	2.236037934668072
5	2.2360679958818954
6	2.2360679774996663
7	2.23606797749979
8	2.23606797749979

Output from secant method

8.5   Exercise 8.1

1.

i.   Estimate   f(0.25)   using interpolating polynomial for the following data

(x (i),f(x(i))= (0.1,0.07972), (0.2,0.1591), (0.3,0.2376)

Using   (h=4)

ii) Define Lagrange Interpolation .

2.
   i.   Write Lagrange interpolating polynomial) $P_n(x)$.

   ii.   Find (interpolating polynomial) P_2 , if we have the values of f(x) on the following points $x=x_0,x_1,x_2$

   iii. Find $P_2(x)$ for f(x) =0,-3,4 x=1,-1,2

3.   Estimate   Y (0)   using interpolating polynomial for the following data.

x_i	2	4	1
y_i	-1	0	4

4.

   i.   Write bisection method algorithm to find the root of f(x)=0 between $[x_0,x_1]$ start with $x_0<x_1,$ $y_0=f(x_0)$

$y_1=f(x_1)$, $y_0y_1<0$ with an error $\varepsilon >0$

ii. Using bisection method find the root of $x^2-2=0$, in the interval $[x_0=0, x_1=2]$ using 3 iterations.

5.   Take 4 steps of the bisection method to estimate a root of $\sin x-0.5 = 0$
starting with the intervals (a) $[0, 1]$ and (b) $[2, 3]$. Estimate the error in the result.

8.6   Exercise 8.2

1.   Apply the Trapezoidal Rule to approximate definite integral

$$\int_0^1 \sqrt{1-x^2}\,dx$$

for n= 10.

2.   Apply the Trapezoidal Rule to the definite integral

$$\int_0^1 \frac{1}{x^2+1}\,dx$$

for n= 10..

3.   Estimate $\int_0^1 (1+X)^{-1}\,dX$

Using the following methods:
i.   Simpson method with 4 sub-intervals.
ii.   Trapezium rule with 4 sub-intervals.
iii.   Write the general Trapezium
    Algorithm for estimating f(x) if

$$\int_a^b f(x)\,dx \approx \frac{h}{2}\left[f(x_0) + f(x_n) + 2\sum_{i=1}^{n-1} f(a+ih) \right]$$

4. Write an algorithm to illustrate Riemann Sums. If we have
y = f(x), interval [a,b] and subinterval n, find the following
Riemann Sums:

1.   left-hand endpoints
2.   right-hand endpoints
3.   midpoints

5. Use the Trapezoidal and Simpson's rules for single intervals to approximate the following integrals. Compare these approximations with the actual value and use the error estimate to find an upper bound for the error in each case.

a) $\displaystyle\int_{1}^{2} \ln x\, dx$

b) $\displaystyle\int_{0}^{0.1} x^{1/3}\, dx$

c) $\displaystyle\int_{0}^{\pi/3} \sin^2 x\, dx$

6. Use Trapezoidal Rule with 4 sub-intervals to estimate

$$\int_{0}^{1} x^{3}\, dx$$

7. Use Simpson method with 4 sub-intervals to estimate

$$f(x) = \int_0^1 \frac{dx}{1+x}$$

8.7   Exercise 8.3

1. Approximate the following integrals.

a) $\displaystyle\int_{0}^{0.1}\sqrt{1+x}\,dx$

b) $\displaystyle\int_{0}^{\pi/2}\sin^{2}x\,dx$

c) $\displaystyle\int_{0}^{1}x^{1/3}x\,dx$

2. Apply Gaussian numerical integration with $n = 2$ to approximate the value of

$$\int_{-1}^{1}\frac{1}{x+3}\,dx = \ln(2)$$

3. Apply Gaussian numerical integration with $n = 2$ to approximate the value of

$$\int_{-1}^{1}\cos(x)\,dx = 2\sin(1)$$

4. Apply Gaussian numerical integration with $n = 3$, the approximate value of the definite integral

$$\int_{-1}^{1}\sqrt{1-x^{2}}\,dx = \pi/2$$

5. Apply Gaussian numerical integration with $n = 5$ to approximate the value of

$$\int_{-1}^{1} \frac{1}{x+3} dx = 1n(2)$$

6. Approximate the value of

$$\int_{-1}^{1} \cos(x) dx = 2\sin(1)$$

using Gaussian numerical integration for the values $n = 1,2,3,4,5$.

7. Using central difference quotient to find the approzimate derivative of
$fx) = \cos(x)$.

For $h = 0. 1, 0. 01, 0. 001,$ and $0. 0001,$ and $x = 0.8$.

Compare with the true value $f(0.8) = \sin(0.8)$.

9   Solution to exercises

9.1   Exercise 1

1.   The number 39 can be expressed in terms of powers of 2 as:
       $1*32 + 0*16 + 0*8 + 1*4 + 1*2 + 1*1$
       which is
       $(1* 2^5) + (0* 2^4) + (0* 2^3) + (1* 2^2) + (1* 2^1) + (1* 2^0)$
       So, the answer is: 100111

2.   The number 98 can be expressed in terms of powers of 2 as:
       $1*64 + 1*32 + 0*16 + 0*8 + 0*4 + 1*2 + 0*1$
       which is
       $(1* 2^6) + (1* 2^5) + (0* 2^4) + (0* 2^3) + (0* 2^2) + (1* 2^1) + (0* 2^0)$
       So, the answer is: 1100010

3.   The number 10011 in base 2 represents:
       $(1* 2^4) + (0* 2^3) + (0* 2^2) + (1* 2^1) + (1* 2^0)$
       which is
       $1*16 + 0*8 + 0*4 + 1*2 + 1*1$
       So, the answer is: 19

4.   Converting the decimal number 1.0 into binary arithmetic:
       The number 1 can be expressed in terms of powers of 2 as:
       $1*1$ which is $(1* 2^0)$
       so, the answer is: 1

5.   11.11100110011001101

6.

In[1]:= **BaseForm** ⌊5, 2⌋⌊____⌋

Out[1]//BaseForm=

0.1_2

7.

In[2]:= **BaseForm** ⌊25, 2⌋ ⌊____⌋

Out[2]//BaseForm=

0.01_2

8.

In[3]:= **BaseForm** ⌊75, 2⌋ ⌊____⌋

Out[3]//BaseForm=

0.11_2

9. 2 3 4 5 6 7 8 9 10 11 12 13 14 15.
Now cross out all the even ones larger than 2:
2 3 4 5 6 7 8 9 ~~10~~ 11 ~~12~~ 13 ~~14~~ 15.
Now cross out all those divisible by 3 (other than 3):
2 3 4 5 6 7 8 ~~9~~ ~~10~~ 11 ~~12~~ 13 ~~14~~ ~~15~~.
So, the numbers 2, 3, 5, 7, 11, and 13 are prime.

10. The exact value of $f(0.001) = 0.001000225$.
For 4-digit chopping we have:
fl ($\sqrt{1.001}$) – fl($\sqrt{0.999}$) = 1.000 – 0.9994 = 0.0006
Relative error is 40%.
Here the cancellation of errors is apparent.
To avoid such cancellation, we use a better relation for $f(x)$
as follows:
$$F(x) = \frac{(\sqrt{1+x} - \sqrt{1-x})(\sqrt{1+x} + \sqrt{1-x})}{(\sqrt{1+x} + \sqrt{1-x})}$$

$$= \frac{2x}{(\sqrt{1+x}+\sqrt{1-x})}$$

Using 4 digit chopping we have:

$f(0.001) = 2(.001) / (fl(\sqrt{1.001}) + fl(\sqrt{0.999}))$

$= 0.002/fl(1.9994) = fl(1.000500 \times 10^{-3}$

$= .001$

Relative error = .02%. No cancellation errors in this case.

11. Result is: **a. 00111010**

11	CARRIES
00011110	$= 30_{(base\ 10)}$
+00011100	$= 28_{(base\ 10)}$
00111010	$= 58_{(base\ 10)}$

     b. **0001011**

1	BORROWS
0010001	$= 17_{(base\ 10)}$
− 0000110	$= 6_{(base\ 10)}$
0001011	$= 11_{(base\ 10)}$

12. Result is: a. **0001000110**

0001010	$= 10_{(base\ 10)}$
× 0000111	$= 7_{(base\ 10)}$
0001010	
0001010	
00001010	
0001000110	$= 70_{(base\ 10)}$

     b. 100

	1 0 0	$= 7_{(base\ 10)}$
1 1 1| 11100		$= 28_{(base\ 10)}$
− 111		$= 4_{(base\ 10)}$
000		

9.2   Exercise 2

1.

   i.   Y+A = the set of all books written either in French or in Arabic.

   ii. RB` = the set of red books

   iii. A (B+R) = the set of all books written in Arabic.

   iv. B+BR = the set of black books and black books written in English.

2.

   i.   AC

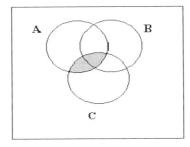

   ii. A+BC

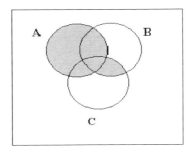

   iii. (A+B)(A+C)

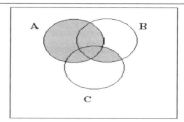

3.

    i.   A+A`BC

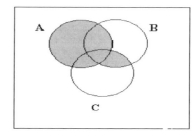

    ii.   (A+B`)(A`+C)

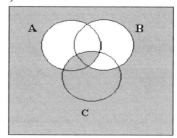

4.   (X+Y)(Z`+W) = (X+Y)Z`+ (X+Y)W   by distributive laws
                        = Z` (X+Y) + W(X+Y) by commutative laws
                        = Z`X+ Z`Y) + WX+WY by distributive laws

5.   AC+AD+BC+BD= A(C+D) + B(C+D) by distributive laws
         = (A+B)(C+D) by distributive laws and commutative laws

6.   X(X`+Y)+ Y(Y+Z) + Y
         = XX`+XY+Y(Y+Z)+Y by distributive laws
         = 0+XY+Y(Y+Z)+Y   by complementation law
         = XY+Y(Y+Z) +Y   by operation with 0 and 1
         = XY+Y+Y   by absorption law
         = XY+Y   by tautology laws
         = Y   by absorption law

9.3   Exercise 3

1.   There are five ways the numbers {1,2,3} can be partitioned:
{{1},{2},{3}}{{1,2},{3}} {{1,3},{2}} {{1},{2,3}}
{{1,2,3}} = 5 ways.

2.   Define the notation as follows:

P(English books): P(E)=.25
P(Arabic books): P(A)=.3
P(Arabicbooks given English books): P(A\E)=.6

a)   Combine the probabilities

$$P(E \cap A) = P(E) \text{ X } P(A \backslash E)$$

$$= .25 \text{ X } .55 = .1375$$

b)   The question is asking for the probability of having the S, given that the student has the A.
We need to re-arrange

$$P(E \cap A) = P(E) \text{ x } P(E \backslash A)$$
$$P(E \backslash A) = P(E \cap A) / P(A)$$
$$= .1375 / .3 = .04125$$

c) Find P(E∩A`)

$$P(A` \backslash E`) = 1 - P(A \backslash E)$$
$$= 1 - .55 = .45$$

$$P(E \cap A`) = .25 \text{ X } .3 = .075$$

d) $P(A \cap E) + P(A \cap E`) + P(A` \cap E) + P(A` \cap E`) = 1$

   $P(E`\backslash A) = 1 - .04125 = .95875$

3.   The probability that the first ball will be selected is 6/45 .
     Assuming that the first ball is good, there will now be 44 balls,
     5 of which are yours. The probability of the second ball also
     being one of yours, is therefore 5/44
     This continues for each ball that is chosen. If we continue to
     be successful, then both the total number of balls and the
     number of our balls, is reduced by one for each draw. The
     probability of all 6 balls being good, is therefore given by
        6/45 x 5/44 x 4/43 x 3/42 x 2/41 x 1/40 = 1/ 8145060

     Probability to win is = 1/8145060
     The next problem is to find the probability of getting 5 balls in
     the main draw, plus the bonus ball. Again we should just
     consider our 6 balls as 6 identical balls. We do not care which
     order they appear, or even which the bonus ball is.
     In this case, we must draw one blue ball in the main draw.
     One possibility is that the first ball is blue and the remaining 5
     are red. The probability of starting with a blue ball is 39/45
     If this happens, we will now have 48 balls left, 6 of which are
     red. The probability of getting a red ball next, is therefore 6/44.

     We must now continue to be successful with each pick, so as
     above, both the total number of balls and the number of red
     balls (the numerator) must reduce by one each time. We can
     therefore say that the probability of a blue ball, followed by 5
     red balls is

$$39/45 \times 6/44 \times 5/43 \times 4/42 \times 3/41 \times 2/40 = 13/2715020$$

However, we are equally likely to get the blue ball second, third, etc... Since there are 6 possible positions for the blue ball, we must multiply our result by 6, to find the probability of getting 5 balls in the main draw
Therefore

$$P(5 balls) = 6 \times 13/2715020 = 39/1357510$$

We now just need to multiply this by the probability of drawing the bonus ball. Remember that we now have 43 balls, only one of which is ours

$$P(5 \ balls + bonus) = 39/1357510 \times 1/39 = 1/1357510$$

4. $P(B) = 2/3$ and $P(A \cap B) = 7/15$

5.   The probability would be $= P(F \ or \ D)$, where F stands for female and D stands for director. In this case the events are non-mutually exclusive because it is possible to be both a female and a director. Thus we use the addition rule as follows:
$P(F \ or \ D) = P(F) + P(D) - P(F \ and \ D) = 20/100 + 15/100 - 5/100 = 30/100 = 0.3.$

9.4   Exercise 4

1.   A closed sentence is a statement which is either true or false.
Statements 1 and 2 are true. Number 3 is false. All are
closed sentences.

2.

An **open sentence** is a statement which contains a variable
and becomes either true or false depending on the value that
replaces the variable
All the sentences are open sentences.

3.   The variable is x in the first sentence, y in the second one
and "he." in the 3rd one. Sentence 1 is true if x is replaced by
7, but false if x is replaced by a number other than
7. Sentence 2 is true if y is replaced by 7, but false
otherwise. Sentence 3 is either true or false depending on the
value of the variable "he."

4.   The **negation** of statement p is "not p." The negation of p
is symbolized by "~p." The truth value of ~p is the
opposite of the truth value of p.
~p mean `the number 8 is not even`, which is a false
statement.

5.

y	~y
T	F
F	T

Here, when y is true, ~y is false; and when y is false, ~y is
true. From this truth table, we can see that a statement and
its negation have opposite truth values.

6.   A **conjunction** is a compound statement formed by joining two statements with the connector AND. The conjunction "p and q" is symbolized by p∧q. A conjunction is true when both of its combined parts are true; otherwise it is false.

7.

p	q	p∧q
T	T	T
T	F	F
F	T	F
F	F	F

8.   Since each statement given represents an open sentence, the truth value of r∧s will depend on the value of variable x. But there are an infinite number of replacement values for x, so we cannot list **all** truth values for r∧s in a truth table. We can, however, find the truth value of r∧s for given values of x as follows:

If x = 3, then r is true, s is true. The conjunction r∧s is true. If x = 9, then r is true, s is false. The conjunction r∧s is false. If x = 2, then r is false, s is true. The conjunction r∧s is false. If x = 6, then r is false, s is false. The conjunction r∧s is false.

9.   1.

x	y	x∧y

T	T	T
T	F	F
F	T	F
F	F	F

2.

x	y	~x	~x ∧ y
T	T	F	F
T	F	F	F
F	T	T	T
F	F	T	F

3.

x	y	~y	~y ∧ x
T	T	F	F
T	F	T	T
F	T	F	F
F	F	T	F

9.5   Exercise 5.1

1. $A + B = B + A$ Additive commutativity

      $A (B + C) = AB + AC$ Distributivity

2. $(AB)C = \begin{pmatrix} 5 & 4 \\ 11 & 6 \end{pmatrix} \begin{pmatrix} 1 & 1 \\ 2 & 0 \end{pmatrix} = \begin{pmatrix} 13 & 5 \\ 23 & 11 \end{pmatrix}$

      $A (BC) = \begin{pmatrix} 1 & 2 \\ 3 & 4 \end{pmatrix} \begin{pmatrix} -3 & 1 \\ 8 & 2 \end{pmatrix} = \begin{pmatrix} 13 & 5 \\ 23 & 11 \end{pmatrix}$

      Therefore $(AB) C = A (BC)$

      $A(B+C) = \begin{pmatrix} 1 & 2 \\ 3 & 4 \end{pmatrix} \begin{pmatrix} 2 & -1 \\ 4 & 3 \end{pmatrix} = \begin{pmatrix} 10 & 5 \\ 22 & 9 \end{pmatrix}$

      $AB + AC = \begin{pmatrix} 5 & 4 \\ 11 & 6 \end{pmatrix} \begin{pmatrix} 5 & 1 \\ 11 & 3 \end{pmatrix} = \begin{pmatrix} 10 & 5 \\ 22 & 9 \end{pmatrix}$

      Therefore $A (B+C) = AB+AC$

3.
$$\alpha A = \begin{bmatrix} \alpha a_{11} & \alpha a_{12} & ... & \alpha a_{1n} \\ \alpha a_{21} & \alpha a_{22} & ... & \alpha a_{2n} \\ ... & ... & ... & ... \\ \alpha a_{m1} & \alpha a_{m2} & ... & \alpha a_{mn} \end{bmatrix}$$

$$\alpha B = \begin{bmatrix} \alpha b_{11} & \alpha b_{12} & ... & \alpha b_{1n} \\ \alpha b_{21} & \alpha b_{22} & ... & \alpha b_{2n} \\ ... & ... & ... & ... \\ \alpha b_{m1} & \alpha b_{m2} & ... & \alpha b_{mn} \end{bmatrix}$$

$\alpha A + \alpha B = C$

$\alpha\, a_{ij} = \alpha a_{ij}\ \ ,\ \alpha\, b_{ij} = \alpha b_{ij}\ \ ,\ \ c_{ij} = sum(\alpha a_{ij} + \alpha\, b_{ij})$ (1)

$$A = \begin{bmatrix} a_{11} & a_{12} & ... & a_{1n} \\ a_{21} & a_{22} & ... & a_{2n} \\ ... & ... & ... & ... \\ a_{m1} & a_{m2} & ... & a_{mn} \end{bmatrix}$$

$$B = \begin{bmatrix} b_{11} & b_{12} & ... & b_{1n} \\ b_{21} & b_{22} & ... & b_{2n} \\ ... & ... & ... & ... \\ b_{m1} & b_{m2} & ... & b_{mn} \end{bmatrix}$$

$A + B = D$

$d_{ij} = sum(a_{ij} + b_{ij})\ \ ,\ \ \alpha\, d_{ij} = sum(\alpha a_{ij} + \alpha b_{ij})$ (2)

From (1) & (2) D=C

4. Follow similar approach as above.

5. AB is incompatible. BA= $\begin{pmatrix} 5 & 5 & 5 \\ 14 & 8 & 8 \end{pmatrix}$, AC= $\begin{pmatrix} 1 & 10 \\ -2 & 10 \end{pmatrix}$

CA= $\begin{pmatrix} 5 & 0 & 0 \\ 10 & 5 & 5 \\ 3 & 1 & 1 \end{pmatrix}$

6. We have, $AA^{-1}=I$ and $A^{-1}A=I$
Then $AA^{-1}A=AI$
$\qquad\qquad IA= AI$ and

7. $A^{-1} = \begin{pmatrix} -2 & 1 \\ 3/2 & -1/2 \end{pmatrix}$

9.6   Exercise 5.2

1. det A= 3+8+0-0-4-2=5
2. det B=ad+cd –cb-cd=ad-cb=det A.
3. det B=akd-bkc=k(ad-bc)=k(det A)
4. Since $I_2 = \begin{pmatrix} 1 & 0 \\ 0 & 1 \end{pmatrix}$, det($I_2$)= 1
5. Expanding the minors using the first row we have:

$$3\begin{pmatrix} 4 & 3 \\ 1 & 2 \end{pmatrix} -0+2\begin{pmatrix} 1 & 4 \\ 2 & 1 \end{pmatrix} =3(8\text{-}3) +2(1\text{-}8) =1$$

9.7   Exercise 6

1. $x_1=1/2$, $x_2=0$, $x_3z=-1$

2. $x_1=82/19$, $x_2=-9/19$

3. $x_1=11/5$, $x_2=-4/5$

4. $$\begin{bmatrix} 3 & 2 \\ 2 & -5 \end{bmatrix}\begin{bmatrix} x_1 \\ x_2 \end{bmatrix}=\begin{bmatrix} 12 \\ 11 \end{bmatrix},\ \begin{bmatrix} 1 & -1 \\ 2 & 3 \\ 3 & 2 \end{bmatrix}\begin{bmatrix} x_1 \\ x_2 \end{bmatrix}=\begin{bmatrix} 3 \\ 2 \\ 5 \end{bmatrix}$$

5. $D=\begin{vmatrix} 3 & 1 \\ 2 & -1 \end{vmatrix}=-5$, $D_{x1}=\begin{vmatrix} 10 & 1 \\ 5 & -1 \end{vmatrix}=-15$, $D_{x2}=\begin{vmatrix} 3 & 10 \\ 2 & 5 \end{vmatrix}=-5$

    $x_1=-15/-5 = 3$, $x_2=-5/-5=1$

9.8   Exercise 7

1.   A vector quantity has a direction and magnitude.

2.   Quantities that have magnitude and no direction.

3.
$$\text{v+u=}\begin{bmatrix} v_1 + u_1 \\ v_2 + u_2 \end{bmatrix}$$

4.   A zero vector is a vector that has magnitude 0 and any direction.

5. $\alpha \, \text{v} = \begin{bmatrix} \alpha v_1 \\ \alpha v_2 \end{bmatrix}$

9.9   Exercise 8.1

1.

i.
$$L_i(x) = \prod_{j}^{n} \frac{x - x_j}{x_i - x_j}$$

$L_0(x) = (x-4)(x-1)/(2-4)(2-1) = -1/2(x-4)\,(x-1)$

$L_1(x) = (x-2)(x-1)/(4-2)(4-1) = (x-2)\,(x-1)3/2$

$L_2(x) = (x-2)(x-4)/(1-2)(1-4) = (x-2)\,(x-4)/3$

$P(x) = -L_0(x)+0L_1(x)+4L_2(x) = 2(x-4)(x-1)+ (x-2)(x-4)\,4/3$

$f(0.25) = -1/2(0.25-4)\,(0.25-1)+(0.25-2)(0.25-4)4/3 = $

10.15625

ii. Lagrange Interpolation is a method to find $p \in P_n$ to
complete the following data

$$X_0\ X_1\ \ldots\ldots\ X_n$$
$$Y_0\ Y_1\ \ldots\ldots\ Y_n$$

$$P_n(x) = \sum_{i=1}^{n} L_i(x) f(x_i)$$

Where $L_i(x) = \prod_{j=0,\,j\neq i}^{n} \dfrac{x - x_j}{x_i - x_j}$

2.

i.
$$\sum_{i=1}^{n} L_i(x) f(x_i) = P_n(x)$$

ii.
$$P_2 = L_0(x)f(x_0) + L_1(x)f(x_1) + L_2(x)f(x_2).$$

iii. $L_0(x) f(x_0) = 0$, $L_1(x) f(x_1) = -3(1/6) (x-1)(x-2)$, $L_2(x) f(x_2) =$
(1/3) $(x-1)(x+1)$,
$P_2 = -3(1/6) (x-1)(x-2) + (1/3) (x-1)(x+1)$

3.

$$L_i(x) = \prod_{j}^{n} \frac{x - x_j}{x_i - x_j}$$

$L_0(x) = (x-4)(x-1)/(2-4)(2-1) = -1/2(x-4)(x-1)$

$L_1(x) = (x-2)(x-1)/(4-2)(4-1) = 1/6(x-2)(x-1)$

$L_2(x) = (x-2)(x-4)/(1-2)(1-4) = 1/3(x-2)(x-4)$

$P(x) = -L0(x) + 0L1(x) + 4L2(x) = 1/2(x-4)(x-1) + 4/3(x-2)(x-4)$

$f(0) = 1/2(0-4) (0-1) + 4/3(0-2)(0-4) = 2 + 32/3 = 38/3$

4.

i.   Repeat
$X_2 := (x_0 + x_1)/2$
$Y_2 := f(x_2)$
If $y_1 y_2 < 0$ then $x_0 := x_2$ $y_0 := y_2$
Else $x_1 := x_2$ $y_1 := y_2$
Until $(x_1 - x_2)/2 = \varepsilon$

ii.   Let a lower pound, b upper pound, c middle point
        of interval and f(a), f(c) and f(b) are associated
        function at these points.

n	a	c	b	f(a)	f(c)	f(b)
0	0	1	2	−	−	+
1	1	1.5	2	−	+	+
2	1	1.25	1.5	−	−	+
3	1.25	1.375	1.5	−	−	+
4	1.375	1.4375	1.5	−	+	+
5	1.375	1.40625	1.4375	−	−	+

Approximate root $c_4 = 1.40625$
The root lies in $\{1.375, 1.4375\}$.
The error in the approximation is:
$\frac{1}{2}(b_4 - a_4) = 1/2(1.4375 - 1.375) = 0.0625$

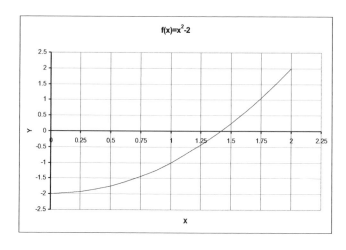

$f(x) = x^2 - 2$

5.

a	c	b	f(a)	f(c)	f(b)
0	0.5	1	-	-	+
0.5	0.75	1	-	+	+
0.5	0.625	0.75	-	+	+
0.5	0.5625	0.625	-	+	+
0.5	0.53125	0.5625	-	+	+

This is interpreted as 4 steps - 4 intervals calculated. Root estimate is midpoint at last step:
0.53125. Error estimate is half interval size: $0.5(0.5625-0.5) = 1/32$.

a	c	b
2	2.5	3
...	...	...
2.5625	2.59375	2.625

Again, this is interpreted as 4 steps. Root estimate is midpoint at last step: 2.59375. Error estimate is half interval size: $1/32$.

Error estimate is upper limit on absolute error.

9.10 Exercise 8.2

1.   The value of the integral is $\pi/4 = 0.785398163$ and
         approximating the value T_n of the definite integral,

$$\int_0^1 \sqrt{1-x^2}\,dx$$

for n=10 we have,

h=(1-0)/10=0.1,

n	x_i	y_i
0	0	1
1	0.1	0.99498744
2	0.2	0.9797959
3	0.3	0.9539392
4	0.4	0.91651514
5	0.5	0.8660254
6	0.6	0.8
7	0.7	0.71414284
8	0.8	0.6
9	0.9	0.43588989
10	1	1.4901E-08

T_n
=(1/20)*(1+2*(0.99498744)+2*(0.9797959)+2*(0.9539392)+2*(0.91651514)+2*(0.8660254)+2*(0.8)+2*(0.71414284)+2*(0.6)+2*(0.43588989) + 1.4901E-08)=0.776129582

Error=0.00926858

2.   Appling the Trapezoidal Rule to the definite integral

$$\int_0^1 \frac{1}{x^2+1} dx$$

we have,

for n=10 we have,

h=(1-0)/10=0.1,

n	x_i	y_i
0	0	1
1	0.1	0.99009901
2	0.2	0.96153846
3	0.3	0.91743119
4	0.4	0.86206897
5	0.5	0.8
6	0.6	0.73529412
7	0.7	0.67114094
8	0.8	0.6097561
9	0.9	0.55248619
10	1	0.5

T_n
=(1/20)*(1+2*(0.99009901)+2*(0.96153846)+2*(0.91743119)+2*(0.86206897)+2*(0.8)+2*(0.73529412)+2*(0.67114094)+2*(0.6097561)+2*(0.55248619)+0.5)= **0.784981497**

3.   Estimating

$$\int_{0}^{1}(1+X)^{-1}dX$$

i.   Simpson's method with 4 subintervals
h= (1-0)/4=1/4

X	F(x)
0	1/(1+0)
¼	1/(1+1/4)
½	1/(1+1/2)
¾	1/(1+3/4)
1	1/(1+1)

$$\int_{0}^{1}(1+X)^{-1}dX = (1/4)/3[1+4(4/5)\ +2(2/3)\ +4(4/7)\ +1/2]$$

$$=1/12[1+16/5+4/3+16/7+1/2]=0.693253$$

ii. Trapezium's method with 4 subintervals
h= (1-0)/4=1/4

X	F(x)
0	1/(1+0)
¼	1/(1+1/4)
½	1/(1+1/2)
¾	1/(1+3/4)
1	1/(1+1)

$$\int_{0}^{1}(1+X)^{-1}dX =1/8[1+2(4/5)\ +2(2/3)\ +2(4/7)\ +1]$$

$$=0.580952$$

iii. Trapezium's Algorithm

$$\int_a^b f(x)dx \approx h\left[(f(a)+f(b))/2 + \sum_{i=1}^{n-1} f(a+ih) \right]$$

Read (a,b,n)
    H :=(b-a)/n
    S :={ f (a) +f (b)}/2
    For i=1, n-1 do
        S: =s + f (a+ ih)
    Write (h, s)

4.   The algorithm is:

a.   Subdivide **[a,b]** into **n** subintervals of equal length.
b.   The length of each of these subintervals is

h = (b-a)/n

c.   We will label the endpoints of the subintervals:
           a_0, a_1, a_2, ..., a_n
   where, **a_i = a + ih**

d.   In each of the subintervals **[a_{i-1}, a_i]**, we pick a number x_i

$$x_i = \begin{cases} a_{i-1} \\ a_i \\ 1/2(a_{i-1}+a_i) \end{cases}$$

depending upon whether we want to use left-hand endpoints, right-hand endpoints or midpoints, respectively.

e.   We then form the Riemann Sum,

$$\sum_{i=1}^{n} f(x_i)h$$

f.   Substituting from d. above, we get the Riemann Sums using

o   left-hand endpoints:

$$\sum_{i=1}^{n} f(x_i)h = \sum_{i=1}^{n} f(a_{i-1})h = \sum_{i=1}^{n} f(a+(i-1)h)h$$

which is also equal to

$$\sum_{i=0}^{n-1} f(a+ih)h$$

which is very useful in computations

o   right-hand endpoints:

$$\sum_{i=1}^{n} f(x_i)h = \sum_{i=1}^{n} f(a_i)h = \sum_{i=1}^{n} f(a+ih)h$$

o   midpoints:

$$\sum_{i=1}^{n} f(x_i)h = \sum_{i=1}^{n} f((1/2)(a_{i-1}+a_i))h = \sum_{i=1}^{n} f(a+(i-1/2)h)h$$

5.   problem   exact   Trapezoidal   Simpson

(a)   0.386294. . .   0.346573. .   0.385834. . .
(b)   0.0348119. . . 0.0232079. . . 0.0322961. . .
(c)   0.307092. . .   0.392699. . .   0.305432. . .

Single interval Trapezoidal rule and error term is

$$\int_a^b f(x) = \frac{h}{2}\left(f(a)+f(b)\right) - \frac{h^3}{12}f''(\zeta), \text{h}=b\text{-}a$$

some ζ between a and b. The error satisfies

$$|error| \le \frac{h^3}{12}\max_{a \le \zeta \le b}|f''(\zeta)|$$

The actual error (exact - approximate solution) must be less than or equal to this upper bound.

Upper bound for the trapezoidal Rule error in the three cases is:

(a) $|error| \le \frac{h^3}{12}\max_{1 \le \zeta \le 2}\left|-(\zeta^{-2})\right| = 1/12$

,

(b) $|error| \le \frac{0.1^3}{12}\max_{0 \le \zeta \le 0.1}\left|2/9(\zeta^{-5/3})\right| = \infty$ unbounded

(c) $|error| \le \frac{\pi^3}{27 \times 12}\max_{0 \le \zeta \le \pi/3}\left|4\cos^2(\zeta)-2\right| = \frac{\pi^3 \times 2}{27 \times 12}$

The Simpson Rule results are similar, but use the 4th derivative.

6.   In general

$$\int_a^b f(x)dx \approx T_n = \frac{h}{2}(y_0 + y_1) + \frac{h}{2}(y_1 + y_2) + ... + \frac{h}{2}(y_{n-1} + y_n)$$

$$= \frac{h}{2}(y_0 + 2y_1 + 2y_2 + ... + 2y_{n-1} + 2y_n)$$

$y_i = f(x_i)$

$n = 4$, $h = (1-0)/4 = 1/4$, $y_0 = 0$, $y_1 = 1/64$, $y_2 = 1/8$, $y_3 = 9/64$, $y_4 = 1$.

$$\int_0^1 x^3 dx \approx 1/8(y_0 + 2y_1 + 2y_2 + 2y_3 + y_4) =$$

$1/8(0 + 1/32 + ¼ + 27/32 + 1) = 17/64 = 0.265625$

7.   In general

$$\int_a^b f(x)dx \approx S_n = \frac{h}{3}(y_0 + 4y_1 + 2y_2 + 4y_3 + 2y_4 + ... + 4y_{2n-1} + y_{2n})$$

$n=4$, $h = (1-0)/4$, $y_0 = 1$, $y_1 = 4/5$, $y_2 = 2/3$, $y_3 = 4/7$, $y_4 = 1/2$.
$S_n = (1/12)(1+16/5 + 4/3 + 16/7 + 1/2) = 0.693253$

9.11 Exercise 8.3

1.

	(a)	(b)	(c)
Exact)	0.102459. . .	0.785398. . .	0.75
Trapezoidal	0.102440. .	0.785398. . .	0.5
Simpson	0.102459. . .	0.785398. . .	0.695800. . .
Midpoint	0.102469. . .	0.785398. .	0.793700. .

2. Applying Gaussian numerical integration with $n = 2$ to approximate the value of

$$\int_{-1}^{1} \frac{1}{x+3} dx = \ln(2)$$

The value of this approximation is the value of G_2 for the function $f(x) = 1/(x+3)$. We have

$$G2 = f\left(-\frac{\sqrt{3}}{3}\right) + f\left(\frac{\sqrt{3}}{3}\right)$$

$$= \frac{3}{9-\sqrt{3}} + \frac{3}{9+\sqrt{3}} = 9/13$$

Therefore

$$\int_{-1}^{1} \frac{1}{x+3} dx \approx 9/13$$

with an error of .000839488, to nine decimal places.

3. Applying Gaussian numerical integration with $n = 2$ to approximate the value of

$$\int_{-1}^{1} \cos(x)dx = 2\sin(1)$$

yields $\displaystyle\int_{-1}^{1} \cos(x)dx \approx \cos\left(-\frac{\sqrt{3}}{3}\right) + \cos\left(\frac{\sqrt{3}}{3}\right)$

To nine decimal places, the error of this approximation is .007118314.

4.

$$\int_{-1}^{1} \sqrt{1 - x^2}\, dx = \pi/2$$

is given by

$$\int_{-1}^{1} \sqrt{1 - x^2}\, dx \approx \frac{5}{9}\sqrt{1 - (-\frac{\sqrt{15}}{5})^2} +$$

$$\frac{8}{9}\sqrt{1 - 0^2} + \frac{5}{9}\sqrt{1 - (\frac{\sqrt{15}}{5})^2}$$

The error of this approximation is -.020820931.

5. Gaussian numerical integration with $n = 5$ to approximate the value of the function $f(x) = 1/(x+3)$. Rounded to nine decimal places, $f(x)$ takes on the following values at each of the nodes:

n	x_n	$f(x_n)$
1	-0.906179846	0.477595938
2	-0.538469310	0.406251283
3	0.0	0.333333333
4	0. 538469310	0.282608075
5	0.906179846	0.256004598

Then $G_5 = 0.693147158$ applying equation 8.2.3.3

with an error of -0.000000023.

6. For the function

$$\int_{-1}^{1} \cos(x)dx = 2\sin(1)$$

using Gaussian numerical integration for the values $n = 1,2,3,4,5$. We form a table to provide nine decimal place values of G_n along with the error $(G_n - 2\sin(1))$ for each value of n.

n	G_n	Error
1	2.000000000	-.317058030
2	1.675823655	0.007118314
3	1.683003548	-0.000061578
4	1.682941689	0.000000281
5	1.682941970	-0.000000001

7.   The approximate derivative of

$f(x) = \cos(x)$.

h	D	Sin(.8)	Error
0.1	-0.716161095	-0.717356091	0.001194996
0.01	-0.717344135	-0.717356091	0.000011956
0.001	-0.717355971	-0.717356091	0.000000120
0.0001	-0.717356090	-0.717356091	0.000000001

10 Annex 1

List of axioms and properties in both logical and Boolean symbols for variables x, y and z and a,b,c for Boolean Algebra.

axioms and properties	Logic	Boolean Algebra
Identities	x OR F = x	a + 0 = a
	x AND T = x	a * 1 = a
Boundedness	x OR T = T	a + 1 = 1
	x AND F = F	a * 0 = 0
Commutative	x AND y = y AND x	a * b = b * a
	x OR y = y OR x	a + b = b + a
Associative	(x OR y) OR z = x OR (y OR z)	(a + b) + c = a + (b + c)
	(x AND y) AND z = x AND (y AND z)	(a * b) * c = a * (b * c)
Distributive	x OR (y AND z) = (x OR y) AND (x OR z)	a + (b * c) = (a + b) * (a + c)
	x AND (y OR z) = (x AND y) OR (x AND z)	a * (b + c) = (a * b) + (a * c)
Complement Laws	x OR ~x = T	a + a' = 1
	x AND ~x = F	a * a' = 0
Uniqueness of Complement	x OR y = T, x AND y = F -> y = ~x	a + x = 1, a * x = 0 -> x = a'
Involution	~(~x) = x	(a')' = a
	~F = T	0' = 1
	~T = F	1' = 0
Idempotent	x OR x = x	a + a = a
	x AND x = x	a * a = a
Absorption	x OR (x AND y) = x	a + (a * b) = a
	x AND (x OR y) = x	a * (a + b) = a
DeMorgan's	~(x OR y) = ~x AND ~y	(a + b)' = a' * b'
	~(x AND y) = ~x OR ~y	(a * b)' = a' + b'

11   Annex 2

1.   The Least-Squares Line

The least-squares line uses a straight line

$$y = a + bx$$

to approximate the given set of data, (x_1, y_1), ,(x_2, y_2), ...,(x_n, y_n), where $n \geq 2$.. The best fitting curve $f(x)$ has the least square error, i.e.,

$$\Pi = \sum_{i=1}^{n} \left[y_i - f(x_i) \right]^2 = \sum_{i=1}^{n} \left[y_i - (a + bx_i) \right]^2 = \min.$$

Note that a and b are unknown coefficients while all x_i and y_i are given. To obtain the least square error, the unknown coefficients a and b must yield zero first derivatives.

$$\frac{d\Pi}{da} = 2 \sum_{i=1}^{n} \left[y_i - (a + bx_i) \right] = 0$$

$$\frac{d\Pi}{db} = 2 \sum_{i=1}^{n} x_i \left[y_i - (a + bx_i) \right] = 0$$

Expanding the above equations, we have:

$$\sum_{i=1}^{n} y_i = a \sum_{i=1}^{n} 1 + b \sum_{i=1}^{n} x_i$$

$$\sum_{i=1}^{n} x_i y_i = a \sum_{i=1}^{n} x_i + b \sum_{i=1}^{n} x_i^2$$

The unknown coefficients *a* and *b* are:

$$a = \frac{\left(\sum y\right)\left(\sum x^2\right) - \left(\sum x\right)\left(\sum xy\right)}{\left(n \sum x^2\right) - \left(\sum x\right)^2}$$

$$b = \frac{n\left(\sum xy\right) - \left(\sum x\right)\left(\sum y\right)}{\left(n \sum x^2\right) - \left(\sum x\right)^2}$$

where $\sum \ldots$ stands for $\sum_{i}^{n} \ldots i$.

2.   The Least-Squares Parabola

The least-squares parabola uses a second degree curve

$$y = a + bx + cx^2$$

to approximate the given set of data, (x_1, y_1), , (x_2, y_2), ..., (x_n, y_n), where n ≥ 3. The best fitting curve f(x) has the least square error, i.e.,

$$\Pi = \sum_{i=1}^{n} \left[y_i - f(x_i)\right]^2 = \sum_{i=1}^{n} \left[y_i - (a + bx_i + cx_i^2)\right]^2 = \min.$$

Note that a, b and c are unknown coefficients while all x_i and y_i are given. To obtain the least square error, the unknown coefficients a, b and c must yield zero first derivatives.

$$\frac{d\Pi}{da} = 2\sum_{i=1}^{n}\left[y_i - (a + bx_i + cx_i^2)\right] = 0$$

$$\frac{d\Pi}{db} = 2\sum_{i=1}^{n}x_i\left[y_i - (a + bx_i + cx_i^2)\right] = 0$$

$$\frac{d\Pi}{dc} = 2\sum_{i=1}^{n}x_i^2\left[y_i - (a + bx_i + cx_i^2)\right] = 0$$

Expanding the above equations, we have

$$\sum_{i=1}^{n}y_i = a\sum_{i=1}^{n}1 + b\sum_{i=1}^{n}x_i + c\sum_{i=1}^{n}x_i^2$$

$$\sum_{i=1}^{n}x_iy_i = a\sum_{i=1}^{n}x_i + b\sum_{i=1}^{n}x_i^2 + c\sum_{i=1}^{n}x_i^3$$

$$\sum_{i=1}^{n}x_i^2y_i = a\sum_{i=1}^{n}x_i^2 + b\sum_{i=1}^{n}x_i^3 + c\sum_{i=1}^{n}x_i^4$$

The unknown coefficients a, b and c can be obtained by solving the above linear equations.

3.   The Least-Squares *m*th Degree Polynomials

When using an mth degree polynomial

$$y = a_o + a_1 x + a_2 x^2 + ... + a_m x^m$$

to approximate the given set of data,
$(x_1, y_1), (x_2, y_2), ..., (x_n, y_n), where \quad n \geq m+1$, the best
fitting curve *f(x)* has the least square error, i.e.,

$$\Pi = \sum_{i=1}^{n} \left[y_i - f(x_i) \right]^2 = \sum_{i=1}^{n} \left[y_i - (a_0 + a_1 x_i + ... + a_m x_i^m) \right]^2 = min.$$

Note that $a_0, a_1, ..., a_m$ are unknown coefficients while all x_i
and y_i are given. To obtain the least square error, the
unknown coefficients $a_0, a_1, ..., a_m$ must yield zero first
derivatives.

$$\frac{d\Pi}{da_0} = 2 \sum_{i=1}^{n} \left[y_i - (a_0 + a_1 x_i + a_2 x_i^2 + ... + a_m x^m) \right] = 0$$

$$\frac{d\Pi}{da_1} = 2 \sum_{i=1}^{n} x_i \left[y_i - (a_0 + a_1 x_i + a_2 x_i^2 + ... + a_m x^m) \right] = 0$$

$$\frac{d\Pi}{da_2} = 2 \sum_{i=1}^{n} x_i^2 \left[y_i - (a_0 + a_1 x_i + a_2 x_i^2 + ... + a_m x^m) \right] = 0$$

.
.
.

$$\frac{d\Pi}{da_m} = 2\sum_{i=1}^{n} x_i^{m} \left[y_i - (a_0 + a_1 x_i + a_2 x_i^{2} + ... + a_m x_i^{m}) \right] = 0$$

Expanding the above equations, we have

$$\sum_{i=1}^{n} y_i = a_o \sum_{i=1}^{n} 1 + a_1 \sum_{i=1}^{n} x_i + a_2 \sum_{i=1}^{n} x_i^{2} + ... + a_m \sum_{i=1}^{n} x_i^{m}$$

$$\sum_{i=1}^{n} x_i y_i = a_o \sum_{i=1}^{n} x_i + a_1 \sum_{i=1}^{n} x_i^{2} + a_2 \sum_{i=1}^{n} x_i^{3} + ... + a_m \sum_{i=1}^{n} x_i^{m+1}$$

$$\sum_{i=1}^{n} x_i^{2} y_i = a_o \sum_{i=1}^{n} x_i^{2} + a_1 \sum_{i=1}^{n} x_i^{3} + a_2 \sum_{i=1}^{n} x_i^{4} + ... + a_m \sum_{i=1}^{n} x_i^{m+2}$$

.
.
.

$$\sum_{i=1}^{n} x_i^{m} y_i = a_o \sum_{i=1}^{n} x_i^{m} + a_1 \sum_{i=1}^{n} x_i^{m+1} + a_2 \sum_{i=1}^{n} x_i^{m+2} + ... + a_m \sum_{i=1}^{n} x_i^{2m}$$

The unknown coefficients $a_0, a_1, ..., a_m$ can hence be obtained by solving the above linear equations.

4.   Multiple Regression

Multiple regression estimates the outcomes (dependent variables) which may be affected by more than one control parameter (independent variables) or there may be more than one control parameter being changed at the same time.

An example is the two independent variables x nd y and one dependent variable z in the linear relationship case:

$$z = a + bx + cy$$

For a given data set (x_1,y_1,z_1), (x_2,y_2,z_2), ...(x_n,y_n,z_n), where $n \geq 3$, the best fitting curve $f(x)$ has the least square error, i.e.,

$$\Pi = \sum_{i=1}^{n}\left[z_i - f(x_i,y_i)\right]^2 = \sum_{i=1}^{n}\left[z_i - (a + bx_i + cy_i)\right]^2 = \min.$$

Please note that a, b and c are unknown coefficients while all, x_i, y_i and z_i are given. To obtain the least square error, the unknown coefficients a, b and c must yield zero first derivatives.

$$\frac{d\Pi}{da} = 2\sum_{i=1}^{n}\left[z_i - (a + bx_i + cy_i)\right] = 0$$

$$\frac{d\Pi}{db} = 2\sum_{i=1}^{n}x_i\left[z_i - (a + bx_i + cy_i)\right] = 0$$

$$\frac{d\Pi}{dc} = 2\sum_{i=1}^{n}y_i\left[z_i - (a + bx_i + cy_i)\right] = 0$$

Expanding the above equations, we have

$$\sum_{i=1}^{n} z_i = a\sum_{i=1}^{n} 1 + b\sum_{i=1}^{n} x_i + c\sum_{i=1}^{n} y_i$$

$$\sum_{i=1}^{n} x_i z_i = a\sum_{i=1}^{n} x_i + b\sum_{i=1}^{n} x_i^2 + c\sum_{i=1}^{n} x_i y_i$$

$$\sum_{i=1}^{n} y_i z_i = a\sum_{i=1}^{n} y_i + b\sum_{i=1}^{n} x_i y_i + c\sum_{i=1}^{n} y_i^2$$

The unknown coefficients a, b and c can hence be obtained by solving the above linear equations.

12   Annex 3

Summary of logic Gates   Truth Table

A	B	A•B
0	0	0
0	1	0
1	0	0
1	1	1

AND

A	B	A+B
0	0	0
1	1	1
1	0	1
1	1	1

OR

A	$\bar{A}$
0	1
1	0

NOT

A	B	$\overline{(A•B)}$
0	0	1
0	1	1
1	0	1
1	1	0

NAND

A	B	$\overline{(A+B)}$
0	0	1
0	1	0
1	0	0
1	1	0

NOR

A	B	$A \oplus B$
0	0	0
0	1	1
1	0	1
1	1	1

XOR

A	B	$\overline{(A \oplus B)}$
0	0	0
0	1	1
1	0	1
1	1	1

XNOR

---

13   Annex 4

Properties of basic matrix operations

The following are valid any matrices A, B, C for which the indicated operations are defined and for any scalar α and β.

A + B = B + A   Additive commutativity   5.7.1

Proof of 5.7.1:

let C= A + B <=> $c_{ij} = a_{ij} + b_{ij}$ (1)

let D= B + A <=> $d_{ij} = b_{ij} + a_{ij}$ (2)

from (1) and (2) $c_{ij} = d_{ij}$ => C = D

A + (B + C) = (A + B) + C Additive associativity   5.7.2

(AB)C = A (BC)   Multiplicative associativity   5.7.3

$(\alpha \beta A) = \alpha (\beta A)$ 5.7.4

$\alpha (AB) = (\alpha A) B = A (\alpha B)$ 5.7.5

Proof of 5.7.3:

Let y denote B.C, then

$y_{k,j} = \text{sum}_p \, b_{k,p} . c_{p,j}$ (1)

Let x denote A.Y then

$z_{i,j} = \text{sum}_k \, a_{i,k} . d_{k,j}$ (2)

(1) in (2) gives

$z_{i,j} = \text{sum}_k \, a_{i,k} . (\text{sum}_p \, b_{k,p} . c_{p,j})$

<=> $z_{i,j} = \text{sum}_{k,p} \, a_{i,k} . b_{k,p} . c_{p,j}$

So the element of the ith row and jth column of A(B.C) is

$\text{sum}_{k,p} \, a_{i,k} . b_{k,p} . c_{p,j}$ (3)

Now we calculate the element of the ith row and jth column of (A.B)C as follows:

Let y' denote A.B, then

$y_{i,p}' = \text{sum}_k\ a_{i,k}.b_{k,p}$ (4)

Let x' denote y'C then
$z_{i,j}' = \text{sum}_p\ y_{i,p}'.c_{p,j}$ (5)

(4) in (5) gives
$z_{i,j}' = \text{sum}_p\ (\text{sum}_k\ a_{i,k}.b_{k,p}).c_{p,j}$

$<=>$ $z_{i,j}' = \text{sum}_{k,p}\ a_{i,k}.b_{k,p}.c_{p,j}$

So the element of the ith row and jth column of (A.B)C is
$\text{sum}_{k,p}\ a_{i,k}.b_{k,p}.c_{p,j}$ (6)

From (3) and (6) $=>$ A(B.C) = (A.B)C

A (B + C) = AB + AC Distributivity		5.7.6
(A + B)C = AC + BC		5.7.7
α (A+B) $\bar{=}\alpha$A+αB		5.7.8
(α +β)A=αA+βA		5.7.9

Proof of 5.7.6:
Let Y= A + B $<=>$ $y_{ij} = b_{ij} + c_{ij}$ (1)
Let X denote A.Y then
$x_{i,j} = \text{sum}_k\ a_{i,k}.y_{k,j}$ (2)
(1) in (2) gives
$z_{i,j} = \text{sum}_k\ a_{i,k}.(b_{ij} + c_{ij})$
So the element of the ith row and jth column of AB is
$x_{i,p}' = \text{sum}_k\ a_{i,k}.b_{k,p}$ (3)
So the element of the ith row and jth column of AC is
$y_{i,p}' = \text{sum}_k\ a_{i,k}.c_{k,p}$ (4)
(3) in (4) give $x_{i,p}' + y_{i,p}' = \text{sum}_k\ a_{i,k}.b_{k,p}\ +\ \text{sum}_k\ a_{i,k}.c_{k,p}$

14 References

1. Hwei P. Hsu, (1990), "Linear Algebra"

2. Abram Aronovich Stolyar, (1983), "Introduction to Elementary Mathematical Logic

3. Hao Wang, (....), " Popular Lectures on Mathematical Logic"

4. J. Eldon Whitesitt, (1995), " Boolean Algebra and Its Applications "

5. Alan D. Solomon, (1990), " The Essentials of Boolean Algebra"

6. Robert N. McCullough, (1988), "Mathematics for Data Processing"

9. GM Phillips & PJ Taylor, (1996), "Theory and Applications of Numerical Analysis"

10. W. Gautschi (1997), "Numerical analysis, an introduction" ISBN 0-8176-3895-5 Quin-woodbine USA

11. Stephen Wolfram "Mathematica, a system for doing mathematics by computer" 2nd ed. 1992

14 References

15 End Notes:

1. Prime numbers and their properties were first studied extensively by the ancient Greek mathematicians. By the time Euclid's Elements appeared in about 300 BC, several important results about primes had been proved. In Book IX of the Elements, Euclid proves that there are infinitely many prime numbers. This is one of the first proofs known which uses the method of contradiction to establish a result. The mathematicians of Pythagoras's school (500 BC to 300 BC) were interested in numbers for their mystical and numerological properties. They understood the idea of primality and were interested in perfect and amicable numbers.(A perfect number is one whose proper divisors sum to the number itself. e.g. The number 6 has proper divisors 1, 2 and 3 and $1 + 2 + 3 = 6$, 28 has divisors 1, 2, 4, 7 and 14 and $1 + 2 + 4 + 7 + 14 = 28$. A pair of amicable numbers is a pair like 220 and 284 such that the proper divisors of one number sum to the other and vice versa.)

2. Every integer can be written as a product of primes in an essentially unique way. Euclid also showed that if the number $2n - 1$ is prime, then the number $2n-1(2n - 1)$ is a perfect number. The mathematician Euler (much later in 1747) was able to show that all even perfect numbers are of this form. It is not known to this day whether there are any odd perfect numbers.

3. The field axioms are generally written in additive and multiplicative pairs.

| Name | addition | multiplication |

Commutativity	a+b=b+a	ab=ba
Associativity	(a+b)+c=a+(b+c)	(ab)c=a(bc)
Distributivity	a(b+c)=ab+ac	(a+b)c=ac+bc
Identity	a+0=a=0+a	a.1=a=1.a
Inverses	a+(-a)=0=(-a)+a	$aa^{-1}=1=a^{-1}a$ if $a \neq =0$

4.   Euclid's Theorems

A theorem sometimes called "Euclid's first theorem" or Euclid's principle states that if p is a prime and p/ab, then p/a or p/b (where /means divides). A corollary is that $p/a^n \Rightarrow p/a$ (Conway and Guy 1996). The fundamental theorem of arithmetic is another corollary (Hardy and Wright 1979).

Euclid's second theorem states that the number of primes is infinite. This theorem, also called the infinitude of primes theorem, was proved by Euclid in Proposition IX.20 of the *Elements* (Tietze 1965, pp. 7-9). Ribenboim (1989) gives nine (and a half) proofs of this theorem. Euclid's elegant proof proceeds as follows. Given a finite sequence of consecutive primes 2, 3, 5, ..., p, the number

$$N=2.3.5...p +1 \qquad\qquad (1)$$

known as the ith Euclid number when $p=p_i$ is the ith prime, is either a new prime or the product of primes. If N is a prime, then it must be greater than the previous primes, since one plus the product of primes must be greater than each prime composing the product. Now, if N is a product of primes, then at least one of the primes must be greater than p. This can be shown as follows.

If N is composite and has no prime factors greater than p, then one of its factors (say F) must be one of the primes in the sequence, 2, 3, 5, ..., p. It therefore divides the product

2.3.5...p. However, since it is a factor of N, it also divides N. But a number which divides two numbers a and $b < a$ also divides their difference a-b, so F must also divide

$$N-(2.3.5...p)=(2.3.5...p+1)-(2.3.5...p)=1 \qquad (2)$$

In about 200 BC the Greek Eratosthenes devised an algorithm for calculating primes called the Sieve of Eratosthenes. Sequentially write down the integers from 2 to the highest number n you wish to include in the table. Cross out all numbers >2 which are divisible by 2 (every second number). Find the smallest remaining number >2. It is 3. So cross out all numbers >3 which are divisible by 3 (every third number). Find the smallest remaining number >3. It is 5. So cross out all numbers >5 which are divisible by 5 (every fifth number).

Continue until you have crossed out all numbers divisible by $n^{.5}$, where [x] is the floor function. The numbers remaining are prime. This procedure is illustrated in the above diagram which sieves up to 50, and therefore crosses out primes up to $[50]^{.5}=7$. If the procedure is then continued up to n, then the number of cross-outs gives the number of distinct prime factors of each number.

There is then a long gap in the history of prime numbers during what is usually called the Dark Ages. The next important developments were made by Fermat at the beginning of the 17th Century. He proved a speculation of Albert Girard that every prime number of the form $4n + 1$ can be written in a unique way as the sum of two squares and was able to show how any number could be written as a sum of four squares. He devised a new method of factorising large numbers which he demonstrated by factorising the number $2027651281 = 44021 \times 46061$.

5. Mathematica
    A system for doing mathematics by computer (see reference 11).

6. George Boole (1815) introduced the first systematic treatment of logic and developed the algebraic system known by his name, Boolean algebra.

7. Cantor, (1845-1918), German mathematician who built a hierarchy of infinite sets according to their cardinal number. By one-to-one pairing, he showed that the set of real numbers has a higher cardinal number than does the set of rational fractions. However, he found every class of algebraic numbers has the same cardinal number as the integers. Such considerations led to his *Mengenlehre* (theory of assemblages) and *Manningfaltigkeitslehre* (theory of manifolds). He also invented the
    Cantor's highly original views were vigorously opposed by his contemporaries, especially Kronecker. The attacks contributed to the nervous breakdowns he suffered throughout the final 33 years of his life. Cantor died in a mental institution.

Contents

16   Index

19319193R00132

Made in the USA
Charleston, SC
17 May 2013